Irish
Countryhouse
Cooking

Compiled by Rosie Tinne

WEATHERVANE BOOKS • NEW YORK

CONTENTS

LIST OF CONTRIBUTORS

Mrs Ivan Allen
The Countess of Altamont
Lady Beit
Mrs John Beresford Ash
Mrs Michael Butt
Donna Maria Caraccido
Lady Maureen C. Colin Cooper
Miss Sybil Connolly
Miss Deirdre Cooper
Mrs Francis Cooper
Lady Cusack Smith
Mrs Donald Davies
The Marchioness of Dufferin
   and Ava
Lady Dunally
Lady Dunsany
Lady Farnham
The Madame FitzGerald
Miss Nesta FitzGerald
Viscountess Gormanston 1941
Lady Holmpatrick
Lady Hort
Mrs John Huston
The Countess of Iveagh

Lady Killanin
Mrs Tom Laidlaw
Mrs Desmond Leslie
Mrs Victor McCalmont
Henry McIlhenny Esq
Lady Mahon
Mrs Bill Montgomery
Lord Mountbatten of Burma
The Countess of
   Mount Charles
Mrs Jack Mullion
Mrs Elizabeth O Brien
Lady O'Neill
Mrs Reggie O'Reilly
Lionel Perry Esq
Lady Rathdonnell
The Hon. Mrs Agnew Somerville
Mrs Anthony Stanley Clarke
Lady Stewart
Lady Honor Svejdar
Mrs Derek Tinne
Mrs Nicholas Tinne
Mrs Derek le Poer Trench
Mrs John Williams

EQUIVALENT MEASURES

INGREDIENTS	BRITISH	AMERICAN
Almonds, ground	4 ozs	1 cup
Almonds, blanched, whole	$5\frac{1}{2}$ ozs	1 cup
Apricots, dried	1 lb	3 cups
Breadcrumbs, dry	$3\frac{1}{4}$ ozs	1 cup
Breadcrumbs, fresh	$1\frac{1}{2}$ ozs	1 cup
Butter	$\frac{1}{2}$ lb	1 cup
Cheese, dry, grated	$\frac{1}{2}$ lb	2 cups
Cheese, fresh, grated	$\frac{1}{2}$ lb	$2\frac{1}{4}$ cups
Cheese, Parmesan	4 ozs	1 cup
Cottage Cheese	1 lb	2 cups, firmly packed
Cornstarch (cornflour)	1 tablespoon	1 heaped tablespoon
Cornstarch (cornflour)	1 oz	3 tablespoons
Dates (stoned)	1 lb	2 cups
Flour	1 lb	4 cups
Macaroni, raw	1 lb	3 cups
Milk	1 pint	2 cups
Prunes	1 lb	$2\frac{1}{2}$ cups
Raisins (seedless)	1 lb	$2\frac{1}{2}$ cups
Rice, raw	$\frac{1}{2}$ lb	1 cup
Sugar, granulated	1 lb	2 cups
Sugar, icing confectioner's	1 lb	$3\frac{1}{2}$ cups
Sugar, brown	1 lb	$2\frac{1}{2}$ cups, firmly packed
Sultanas	1 lb	$2\frac{1}{2}$ cups

FLUID MEASURES

BRTISH	AMERICAN
$\frac{1}{2}$ fluid ounce	1 tablespoon (3 teaspoons)
1 cup (20 tablespoons) 10 fl. ozs	1 cup (16 tablespoons) 8 fl. ozs ($\frac{1}{2}$ pint)

All spoons are measured level unless otherwise stated.

FOREWORD

IRELAND has never boasted a reputation for fine food. To most outsiders 'Irish cooking' conjures up a mental picture of mounds of boiled potatoes served with Irish Stew; often they do not realise that this is traditional cottage cooking which, while it can be tasty, rarely takes advantage of the wealth of fresh ingredients available here in Ireland. We are fortunate to have a country which is still relatively unpolluted, with woods full of game and rivers and coastal waters brimming with fish. Yet, rightly or wrongly, these have tended to become the preserves of the better off who, until recently, have also experimented most with growing the less usual vegetables.

It seemed to me wrong that Ireland's gastronomic reputation should rest on cottage cooking, and it was for this reason that I set out to collect recipes from the houses where higher standards have prevailed for many generations, and where superb meals can still be enjoyed today.

A few years ago my husband and I started a small restaurant in Dublin in the hope of making ends meet. Fortunately it has survived, and many of the recipes on Snaffles writing paper are ones we have tried out on our customers. For the rest I am more than grateful to all those people who have so kindly sent me their own recipes and given me permission to use engravings or prints of their houses. In particular I should like to thank Desmond Guinness for his general encouragement and help, and my efficient assistant Deborah Bowyer.

I would like to make it quite clear that, of the engravings featured, the following houses only are open to the public: Castle Coole, Castletown and Carton House. The remainder are private houses.

Unless otherwise stated, all the recipes I have included are *for four people*.

Many feel, as I do, that the image of Irish cooking could be improved and hope, with me, that this book will do something to help.

ROSIE TINNE

SNAFFLES,
47, LOWER LEESON STREET,
DUBLIN 2.
DUBLIN 60790

LOBSTER BISQUE

2 lobster shells — more if possible
1 onion — peeled and cut in half
2 tablespoons tomato purée
2 cloves garlic — skin on
6 peppercorns
pinch saffron
1 heaped tablespoon flour
2 oz butter
sprig thyme
2 tablespoons parsley — chopped
2 pt good fish stock
$\frac{1}{2}$ pt dry white wine
1 dessertspoon salt
$\frac{1}{4}$ pt double cream
1 glass brandy
3 fresh tomatoes — coarsely chopped

Pound lobster shells well in a mortar until fine. Melt butter in a saucepan. Put in shells and flour and brown lightly on a low heat. Add fish stock, wine, onion, garlic, tomato purée, salt, peppercorns, herbs and fresh tomatoes. Simmer gently for 1-1 $\frac{1}{2}$ hours. Add brandy and cook a further 15 minutes. Strain and add cream.

13

Castle Leslie,
Glaslough,
Co. Monaghan.

GLASLOUGH SOUP

1½ pt natural yoghourt
¾ lb potatoes — mashed
1 clove garlic — crushed
4 bunches watercress
1 oz butter
1 tablespoon fresh chives — chopped
salt and pepper to taste

Put yoghourt, potatoes, salt, pepper, garlic and watercress in liquidiser and blend. Warm in saucepan and then add butter and chives.

Helen Leslie

IRISH FISH SOUP

1 cod's head
1 eel
1 mackerel
3 small skate
1 small plaice
2 large onions — finely chopped
3 tablespoons olive oil
1 teaspoon sea salt

good pinch saffron
pinch cayenne pepper
1 teaspoon dried fennel seeds
3 cloves garlic
1 tablespoon parsley — chopped
3 tomatoes — skinned
2 tablespoons tomato paste

SAUCE
2 cloves garlic — crushed
$\frac{1}{2}$ pt mayonnaise
4 teaspoons tomato purée

All fish should be scaled, cleaned and filleted. Use whatever heads are available. Put all the fish heads and backs in a saucepan of cold water to cover, bring to the boil and simmer for 30 minutes. Skim the scum off the top during cooking. Sauté finely chopped onions in hot oil. Mix in a bowl sea salt, saffron, cayenne pepper, fennel seeds, crushed garlic and chopped parsley. Add this to cooked onions and the strained fish stock, mixed with coarsely chopped tomatoes and tomato paste. Bring to boil very quickly, reduce heat and simmer 1 $\frac{1}{2}$ hours. Add fish, cut in medium size chunks, and simmer slowly for 10 minutes until just cooked; do not overcook. Make sauce by mixing crushed garlic with tomato purée and mayonnaise and serve soup in individual bowls with sauce on top.

Castlegar, Galway

CREAM OF CELERY SOUP

1 oz butter
1 lb celery (including leaves) — finely chopped
6 oz onion — finely chopped
½ pt veal or chicken stock
1 pt milk
1 oz cornflour
¼ pt double cream

Sauté ½ lb of celery and onion in butter for 5 minutes. Pour in stock and simmer for 10-15 minutes. Heat ¾ pt milk. Strain soup, add the hot milk and bring to boiling point. Stir in cornflour slaked in the remaining cold milk. Bring to boiling point and let simmer for 1 minute. Just before serving, add the remaining ½ lb of chopped celery and the cream. Simmer for 2 minutes, stirring all the time.

Suzanne Mahon

GAME SOUP

1 oz pale lean bacon — cubed
1 oz butter
1 onion — sliced
1 carrot — sliced
1 stick celery — chopped
1 oz flour
2 pt good stock
1 bouquet garni (thyme, bay leaf, parsley)
1 clove
¼ pt dry sherry
salt and pepper
2 pheasant or wild duck carcases — or more if smaller game

Gently fry bacon in butter with onion, carrot and celery until brown. Add flour and brown. Add stock, carcases and all dry ingredients and simmer gently for 2 hours. Add sherry and cook for further 10 minutes. Check seasoning. Strain and serve.

TRIPE SOUP

1 lb tripe
2 oz carrots
2 oz parsnips
3 oz butter
3 oz flour
salt and pepper
1 clove garlic — crushed
½ teaspoon marjoram — finely chopped
parsley — finely chopped
5 oz cooked ham — chopped

Wash tripe well in cold water, then blanch in boiling water. Wash once more in cold water. Place in pot and cover with cold water (about 2-3 pints). Simmer for ½ hour. When tripe is tender, lift from the liquid and cut into thin strips. Add sliced carrots and parsnips to the liquid and replace tripe. Cook another ½ hour. Melt butter in a frying pan and add flour. When light brown in colour, pour into the soup. Salt to taste. Add garlic, pepper and marjoram. Just before serving, add parsley and ham.

Hana Snyder

IRISH OYSTER SOUP

2 large potatoes
3-4 dozen fresh oysters
¼ lb pork belly — finely diced
1½ pt milk
1 bouquet garni
1½ oz butter
salt and pepper

Peel and boil potatoes and heat the milk. Meanwhile open oysters and put them and liquor in a bowl. Fry the diced pork belly over moderate heat until cooked through. Drain and mash the potatoes in a saucepan, adding hot milk gradually. Add bouquet garni, salt and pepper and bring mixture to the boil. When it boils, add the oysters and their liquor and simmer very gently for 3 minutes. Check seasoning and add butter.

CLEAR CHILLED BORSCH

4 *raw beetroots* — *peeled and grated*
3 *onions* — *grated*
2 *pt good game stock* or *consommé*
1 *teaspoon salt*
pepper to taste
juice 1 *lemon*

FOR GARNISH
1 *tablespoon chives*— *chopped*
sour cream

Put beetroots and onions in saucepan with game stock. Add salt and pepper to taste. Cook quickly for 20 minutes, add lemon juice, checking seasoning. Strain. Float dessertspoon sour cream on top of each bowl and sprinkle with chopped chives.

YOGHOURT SOUP

8 *cartons plain yoghourt*
$\frac{1}{2}$ *pt chicken stock*
$\frac{1}{2}$ *pt tomato juice*
$\frac{1}{2}$ *pt cream*
seasoning to taste

FOR GARNISH
prawns — chopped
cucumber — diced
fresh mint — chopped

Blend all ingredients together and chill. Serve with chopped prawns and diced cucumber and sprinkle with chopped mint.

Betsy Caroline Laidlaw

COLD APPLE AND CURRY SOUP

$1\frac{1}{2}$ *pt good jellied chicken stock*
$\frac{1}{4}$ *pt double cream*
4 *teaspoons curry powder*
$\frac{1}{4}$ *pt apple juice*
1 *tablespoon sherry*
2 *eating apples — finely chopped*
1 *teaspoon fresh lemon juice*

FOR GARNISH
unpeeled green apple — cut into thin strips

Put stock and double cream into saucepan. Heat well but do not boil. Stir in the curry powder and apple juice. Cool the soup, add sherry and chill well. Add chopped apple and lemon juice to the soup. Serve in soup bowls with strips of green apple.

CHEESE SOUP

1 oz flour
1 oz butter
$\frac{1}{4}$ lb parmesan cheese— freshly grated
$\frac{1}{4}$ lb gruyere cheese— freshly grated
1 $\frac{1}{2}$ pt good chicken stock
$\frac{1}{4}$ pt cream
salt and pepper to taste
2 egg whites — stiffly beaten
1 dessertspoon chives or parsley — chopped

Heat butter in saucepan and blend in flour. Add stock. Simmer very slowly for 15 minutes. Add cheese and cream, checking seasoning. Serve individually with beaten egg white and sprinkle with chives or parsley.

ARTICHOKE SOUP WITH RED CAVIAR

5 *jerusalem artichokes — coarsely chopped*
1 ½ *pt good chicken or veal stock*
salt and pepper to taste
1 *medium-sized onion — coarsely chopped*
1 *small potato — coarsely chopped*
¼ *lb butter*
¼ *pt cream*

FOR GARNISH
1 *small jar red caviar*
1 *tablespoon fresh chives — finely chopped*
1 *egg white — stiffly beaten*

Put artichokes, onion and potato into saucepan with butter. Sweat with lid on until soft. Add stock, checking seasoning. Liquidise or sieve. Add cream. Serve hot with egg white placed on top and sprinkled with red caviar and chopped chives.

Foaty Island, Cork

SNAFFLES,
47, LOWER LEESON STREET,
DUBLIN 2.
DUBLIN 60790

CARROT SOUP

5 *young carrots — coarsely chopped*
1 *small onion — coarsely chopped*
1 *small potato — coarsely chopped*
2 *oz butter*
2 *pt good chicken or veal stock*
salt and pepper to taste
$\frac{1}{4}$ *pt cream*

FOR GARNISH
1 *dessertspoon chives — chopped*

Put vegetables and butter in saucepan with lid on, and sweat until soft. Add stock, checking seasoning and simmer for 10 minutes. Sieve or liquidise, add cream and serve with sprinkled chives.

CELERY SOUP WITH TOASTED ALMONDS

1 *head celery*
1 *onion — chopped*
1 *potato — peeled and chopped*
1 *clove garlic — crushed*
2 *sprigs parsley — chopped*
¼ *lb butter*
2 *pt good chicken* or *veal stock*

FOR GARNISH
¼ *pt double cream — whipped*
2 *tablespoons almonds — toasted and chopped*

Remove leaves from celery. Wash thoroughly and chop finely. Sweat celery, potato, onion, garlic and parsley in butter in a saucepan over very low heat until soft. Add stock and bring to boiling point. Check seasoning. Blend in liquidiser or pass through food mill. Heat and serve in soup bowls with blob of whipped cream on each and sprinkled with toasted almonds.

28

DONALD DAVIES OF DUBLIN
CHARLEVILLE LIMITED,
ENNISKERRY, CO. WICKLOW, IRELAND

MELON VINAIGRETTE

2 *chianti* or 1 *cantaloup melon*
1 *lb tomatoes*
½ *cucumber*
3 *avocado pears*
vinaigrette dressing (see page 191)

Skin tomatoes and chop in chunks. Peel cucumber and dice. Scoop out centres of melon(s) and avocado pears with a silver teaspoon. Mix them all together and chill well. Put in individual glasses or china bowls, and before serving add a liberal amount of vinaigrette dressing.

Mary Davies

COLD TOMATO SOUFFLÉ
NELLIE GALLAGHER'S RECIPE

2 *lb ripe tomatoes — skinned and diced*
$\frac{1}{2}$ *pt thick mayonnaise*
1 *small onion — grated*
salt and pepper
4 *leaves gelatine — dissolved in $\frac{1}{2}$ pt warm stock or $\frac{1}{2}$ pt aspic jelly*
$\frac{1}{4}$ *pt cream — whipped*

FOR GARNISH
parsley — chopped

Pass half the tomatoes through sieve, leaving the remainder for decoration. Flavour some thick mayonnaise with grated onion, sieved tomatoes, salt, pepper and add dissolved gelatine or aspic jelly. Add the whipped cream and mix. Put a band of paper round a soufflé dish with a glass in the centre and fill up with the mixture. Put on ice. When ready to serve, fill centre with tomato dice and sprinkle with chopped parsley. Serve with a rich tomato sauce *(see page 199)* with some sour cream added.

Henry P. McIlhenny

AVOCADO PEAR STARTER

2 avocado pears
½ honeydew melon
4 tomatoes — peeled
olive oil
lemon juice or wine vinegar
1 clove garlic — crushed
pinch mixed herbs
salt and pepper
sugar

FOR GARNISH
chopped lettuce
prawns (optional)

Dice avocado pears, melon and tomatoes and over them pour a dressing of 2 parts oil to 1 part lemon juice, seasoned with crushed garlic, herbs, salt, pepper and sugar. Chill for at least 2 hours and serve on a bed of chopped lettuce. Prawns may be added if desired.

Daphne Montgomery

AVOCADO MOUSSE

1 *level tablespoon gelatine*
1 *teaspoon onion juice*
2 *teaspoons worcester sauce*
2-3 *avocado pears (to give about $\frac{3}{4}$ pt pulp)*
$\frac{1}{4}$ *pt mayonnaise*
$\frac{1}{4}$ *pt double cream — lightly whipped*
salt to taste

Soak the gelatine in $\frac{1}{4}$ pt cold water, then dissolve it by heating gently. Peel and crush the avocados with a silver fork. Add to the liquid, with the salt, onion juice and worcester sauce. When cold, fold in the mayonnaise and cream. Pour into an oiled ring mould and leave to set. If desired, the centre of the mousse can be filled with prawns and served with French dressing.

AVOCADO PEARS WITH SOUR CREAM AND CAVIAR

2 ripe avocado pears
juice 1 lemon
4 tablespoons sour cream
4 teaspoons caviar
salt and pepper
4 sprigs parsley

Cut avocados lengthwise. Remove stones and sprinkle flesh with lemon juice to prevent browning. Fill cavity with sour cream which has been seasoned with salt and pepper. Sprinkle each avocado half with caviar. Decorate each with a sprig of parsley.

Howth House, Dublin

SNAFFLES MOUSSE

6 oz cream cheese
6 oz tin beef consommé — undiluted
1 small clove garlic
small pinch curry powder

FOR GARNISH
parsley
1 lemon — cut in wedges

Put all ingredients in a liquidiser and blend until smooth. Fill individual ramekins or 1 soufflé dish and refrigerate until set. Serve with chopped parsley, lemon wedges and hot toast.

YOGHOURT MOUSSE

2 6 oz tins consommé — undiluted·
2¼ pt jars natural yoghourt
1 clove garlic — crushed
pinch cayenne pepper

FOR GARNISH
sour cream — whipped
1 olive

Mix consommé with yoghourt, crushed garlic and a pinch of cayenne pepper. When set, decorate with whipped sour cream and an olive.

Elizabeth A. O Brien

𝔏𝔦𝔰𝔫𝔞𝔳𝔞𝔤𝔥.

ℜ𝔞𝔱𝔥𝔳𝔦𝔩𝔩𝔶

ℑ𝔯𝔢𝔩𝔞𝔫𝔡.

CUCUMBER AND CHEESE MOULD

1 large cucumber — finely diced
6 oz cream cheese
1 teaspoon onion juice
$\frac{1}{4}$ pt chicken stock
$\frac{1}{2}$ oz gelatine soaked in 3 tablespoons cold water
2 tablespoons white wine vinegar
1 tablespoon castor sugar
pinch ground mace
$\frac{3}{4}$ pt cream — lightly whipped
salt and pepper

FOR GARNISH
watercress

Oil a 2-pt ring mould. Sprinkle diced cucumber with salt and leave pressed between 2 plates for 30 minutes. Work cheese into a paste with onion juice and seasoning. Boil stock and pour onto soaked gelatine and, when dissolved, add it to the cheese mixture. Drain cucumber and mix it with vinegar, sugar and mace. When cheese mixture is quite cold, fold in cucumber and cream. Pour into mould and leave to set. Turn out mousse and fill centre with watercress.

Jessica Rathdonnell

GNOCCI DUNSANY

3 oz cheddar cheese
4 eggs
¼ pt milk
2 oz butter
4 large tablespoons cream — whipped
salt and pepper

Grate the cheese and put 2 oz into a saucepan with egg yolks, butter, milk, salt and pepper. Stir all together over a low heat until butter is melted, taking care it does not curdle. Remove from heat and let it stand for a few minutes. Meanwhile whip the egg whites until stiff and fold gently into mixture. Pour into buttered fireproof dish and bake in hot oven (400° F or Gas No. 6) until set (about 20 minutes). Remove from oven and, having cut into squares in dish, cover quickly with whipped cream and the remaining 1 oz of grated cheese. Return to oven for about 4 minutes until slightly brown.

Sheila Dunsany

PÂTÉ AND EGG ASPIC

1 *packet aspic crystals*
½ *lb chicken liver pâté (home made, if possible)*
4 *eggs*
mayonnaise
1 *glass dry sherry*

FOR GARNISH
fresh tarragon — finely chopped

Make aspic jelly using equal parts of sherry and water and the crystals. Poach 1 egg per person, making sure not to overcook — the yolks must be soft. Drain and cool. Pour a little cool aspic jelly into each small bowl and leave to set. Add a dessertspoon of pâté and a little more jelly and allow to set. Finally add the egg, and almost fill with jelly. (The aspic jelly should be warmed slightly to melt before each addition.) Chill well. Put a dessertspoon of mayonnaise on top, and garnish with tarragon.

GOOSE PÂTÉ

1 lb goose meat — minced
½ lb belly of pork — minced
½ lb veal — minced
3 tablespoons brandy
2 cloves garlic — crushed
pinch nutmeg
⅛ pt cider
½ lb thin pale bacon rashers
6 juniper berries — crushed
salt and pepper

Thoroughly mix goose meat, pork and veal. Add crushed garlic, nutmeg, salt and pepper, juniper berries and brandy. Moisten with cider to make a soft mixture. Line a terrine with rindless rashers and fill up with the pâté mixture. Cover with tin foil or lid. Place dish in a pan of water and cook in slow oven until pâté comes away from sides, at least 1½ hours. Remove from oven and put a weight on top of pâté. Leave to cool until next day.

40

TROUT PÂTÉ

$\frac{1}{2}$ *lb smoked trout — filleted*
$\frac{1}{2}$ *lb butter — melted*
3 oz bread (no crusts)
1 teaspoon tomato purée
$\frac{1}{4}$ *pt cream — whipped*
olive oil
paprika
salt

FOR GARNISH
chives or *parsley — chopped*

Moisten bread with a little oil. Put trout, bread, butter and purée in blender and mix thoroughly. Add cream, paprika and salt to taste. Serve in separate pots, decorated with chopped chives or parsley.

Diana Stewart

SNAFFLES,
47, LOWER LEESON STREET,
DUBLIN 2.
DUBLIN 60790

CRAB MOUSSE

1 *tablespoon powdered gelatine*
2 *tablespoons mayonnaise*
2 *tablespoons fresh lime* or *lemon juice*
1 *tablespoon parsley — chopped*
1 *tablespoon French mustard*
salt and pepper
1 *lb crab meat — cooked and flaked*
$\frac{2}{3}$ *pt double cream — whipped*
2 *egg whites — stiffly beaten*

FOR GARNISH
1 *avocado pear — mashed with lemon juice*
1 *tablespoon chives — chopped*

Dissolve gelatine in 3 tablespoons warm water. Mix with mayonnaise, lime or lemon juice, herbs, mustard, salt and pepper to taste. Mix well with crab meat and fold in whipped cream. Chill and when nearly set, fold in egg whites. Pour mixture into an oiled ring mould and chill until set. Unmould the mousse and fill the centre with the avocado mashed with lemon juice and sprinkle with chopped chives.

MACKEREL MOUSSE

3 *baked mackerel — boned and skinned*
1 *glass dry sherry*
6 *oz cream*
$\frac{1}{4}$ *pt mayonnaise*
lots of freshly ground black pepper
salt to taste
1 *clove garlic — squeezed*
1 *shallot — finely chopped*
1 *dessertspoon powdered gelatine*

Put prepared mackerel in liquidiser with sherry, cream, mayonnaise, pepper, salt, garlic and shallot. Liquidise. Melt powdered gelatine in $\frac{1}{4}$ pt warm water. Add to liquidiser and blend. Chill until next day.

SARDINE MOUSSE

2 *large tins sardines*
$\frac{1}{2}$ *pt double cream — lightly whipped*
3 *tablespoons thick béchamel sauce*
3 *sheets leaf gelatine*
paprika
tabasco sauce
salt and pepper

FOR GARNISH
tomato — sliced
cucumber — sliced

Drain the oil from the sardines, remove their backbones and mash them up with a fork. Dissolve the gelatine in a little warm water and put the sardines, béchamel and gelatine into a saucepan and cook for 5 minutes or so, stirring with a wooden spoon. Season well. When the mixture is cold, stir in the whipped cream and whisk until smooth. Transfer the mixture to a soufflé dish and put it in the refrigerator for at least 2 hours before serving. Decorate with tomato and cucumber slices and serve with crisp toast.

PRAWN SOUFFLÉ

3 *eggs*
$\frac{1}{2}$ *pt milk*
$\frac{1}{2}$ *tablespoon powdered gelatine — dissolved*
  in a little warm water
2 *tablespoons cream*
anchovy essence
pinch cayenne pepper
$\frac{1}{2}$ *lb fresh prawns*

Separate eggs. Make custard out of yolks and milk, beaten with cayenne pepper and anchovy essence in saucepan over a low heat. Put in basin and add dissolved gelatine. Stir in cream and set aside until almost cool and set. Add mashed prawns and stiffly beaten egg whites.

Jessica Ratndonnell

Castletown, Kildare

SNAFFLES,
47, LOWER LEESON STREET,
DUBLIN 2.
DUBLIN 60790

MUSSEL PANCAKES

8 pancakes (see page 212)
2 quarts mussels
1 onion — finely chopped
1 shallot — finely chopped
3 oz butter
$2\frac{1}{2}$ tablespoons flour
$\frac{1}{2}$ pt white wine
1 tablespoon parsley — chopped
salt and pepper to taste

Make pancakes in advance *(see page 212)*. Wash mussels very thoroughly, scraping off beards. Place them in a saucepan with $\frac{1}{2}$ pt water and wine and heat until they are just open. Immediately withdraw from heat and drain, reserving liquid; reduce this to $\frac{1}{2}$ pt. Sauté onion and shallot in butter until soft, add flour, then reduced liquid from mussels. Cook very gently for 5 minutes. Season with freshly ground pepper and very little salt. Shell the mussels and add to the mixture. Add the rest of the butter and chopped parsley. Spread each pancake with hot mixture. Roll and place on heated platter. Serve very hot.

PANCAKE COLLEEN

2 oz butter
1 oz onion — finely chopped
3 oz mushrooms — sliced
8 oz shrimps — cooked
8 oz Dublin Bay prawns — cooked
½ glass Irish whiskey
2 tablespoons lobster sauce
  (made as lobster Bisque, see page 13,
  but with half quantity of liquid)
2 tablespoons cream
2 oz cheese — grated
8 thin pancakes (see page 212)

Melt butter in saucepan, then add onion, mushrooms, shrimps, prawns and the Irish whiskey. Add the lobster sauce and cream and simmer for 2 minutes. Fill the pancakes with the mixture and fold. Pour over melted butter and sprinkle with cheese. Brown under hot grill.

Nicola O'Reilly

EGG AND BACON CROQUETTES

4 hard-boiled eggs — coarsely chopped
¾ pt thick cold béchamel sauce
1 egg
1 large onion — coarsely chopped
1 oz butter
4 slices bacon — finely diced
1 large sprig parsley
fine breadcrumbs
salt and pepper

FOR GARNISH
lemon wedges

Sauté onion in butter with bacon. Mix cold eggs with cold béchamel and stir in onion and bacon mixture. Add salt and pepper and chopped parsley. Shape into oval croquettes. Beat fifth egg well. Dip croquettes in egg and roll in breadcrumbs. Chill for at least 2 hours. Fry lightly in smoking deep fat. Serve very hot, garnished with lemon wedges.

SNAFFLES,
47, LOWER LEESON STREET,
DUBLIN 2.
DUBLIN 60790

GULLS' EGGS

12 gulls' eggs — uncooked
3 tablespoons celery salt

Gulls' eggs are in season in May and make a delicious first course. The shells are an attractive speckled pale bluey-green colour. Place eggs in saucepan. Cover with cold water and bring to the boil. Boil for 5 minutes. Remove immediately from heat and plunge in cold water. Serve cold in a basket or bowl or linen napkin in their shells. Each person shells his own eggs and dips them in celery salt. The yolks should be set but not hard.

IRISH EGGS

5 eggs
½ oz butter
1 anchovy
6 capers
pinch parsley — finely chopped
pinch chives — finely chopped
*   or ½ small shallot*
salt, pepper and nutmeg to taste

Melt the butter in an ovenproof dish suitable for table. Break 3 eggs on it. Beat up the yolks of the other 2 eggs. Mince the anchovy and capers very finely. Add the parsley and chives (or chopped shallot), together with salt, pepper and nutmeg. Mix together thoroughly with the yolks. Whisk the 2 egg whites, fold them into other ingredients and pour over the eggs on the dish. Place in a hot oven, so that the eggs may set quickly. 3 minutes should suffice to cook the eggs, which should not be at all hard.

Pamela Gormanston

EGGS AU GRATIN
MAY A. CARROLL'S RECIPE

3 oz butter
6 mushrooms
4 hard-boiled eggs
½ pt béchamel sauce (made with ¾ oz butter, ¾ oz flour, ½ pt milk)
4 oz cheese — grated

Sweat the mushrooms in 1 oz butter for 3 minutes. Shell eggs, remove yolk and mix well with chopped mushrooms. Add the remaining butter, stir well and refill the cavities of the whites with mixture. Place on shallow gratin dish, cover with béchamel sauce mixed with cheese. Bake in a hot oven until brown on top.

SCRAMBLED EGG WITH IRISH SMOKED SALMON

12 eggs
2 oz butter
⅓ lb smoked salmon — sliced
salt and pepper

Mix eggs well, seasoning with salt and pepper. Put saucepan in a pan of hot water, and stir mixture well until eggs begin to coagulate. Add butter bit by bit, stirring all the time. When eggs have a creamy consistency, put immediately on heated platter and cover with slices of smoked salmon. Serve immediately. This is a very good lunch or supper dish served with a green salad.

Russborough, Wicklow

EGGS MESSINE

4 *eggs*
6 *tablespoons lightly cooked rice*

SAUCE MESSINE

½ *pt cream*	1 *lemon*
2 *oz butter*	1 *teaspoon French mustard*
1 *teaspoon flour*	1 *teaspoon fresh tarragon*
2 *egg yolks*	1 *teaspoon fresh chervil*
2 *shallots* or *small onions — chopped*	1 *teaspoon fresh parsley*

Plunge the eggs in their shells into boiling water. The water will stop boiling. Count 6 minutes from the time the water comes to the boil again. Then plunge them immediately into a bowl of cold water. Peel them very carefully and lay them on a bed of lightly cooked rice in a shallow dish. Keep the dish warm, and immediately before serving cover them with warm Sauce Messine, made as follows:

Mix chopped herbs and shallots with 1 teaspoon of grated lemon rind. Work the butter and flour together, add mustard and combine with the herb mixture, egg yolks and cream. Gently heat this mixture in a double saucepan, stirring all the time. Do not allow to boil. Squeeze in the juice of the lemon, and keep stirring until well blended.

Sauce Messine is delicious served with fillets of sole which have been poached in milk or in fish stock, and then drained before placing in the dish lined with rice, exactly as for the soft-boiled eggs.

Clementine Beit

OEUFS À LA GERALDINE

6 hard-boiled eggs — coarsely chopped
2 6 oz tins prawns
1 10 oz tin asparagus
½ pt cream — lightly whipped
2 oz butter
1 tablespoon chervil — chopped
1 tablespoon parsley — chopped
1 teaspoon French mustard
1 cup cheese — grated
salt and black pepper

Put chopped eggs in a bowl and add prawns, salt and pepper to taste and chervil and parsley. (If chervil is unavailable, double the quantity of parsley.) Melt butter and stir in mustard. Blend this into the egg mixture. Fold in cream. Spoon mixture into small fireproof dishes, one for each person, lay 2 or 3 asparagus spears on each dish and cover with grated cheese. Put in hot oven for a few minutes until the cheese is melted and the eggs are heated through. This dish is good for 'starters' but also makes a good main course, using twice as many eggs and heating in one large dish.

COUNTRY EGGS

1 *lb potatoes — peeled*
3 *oz butter*
3 *oz gruyère cheese — grated*
8 *eggs*
$\frac{1}{4}$ *pt double cream*
salt and pepper

Cut potatoes into very thin rounds. Slowly cook potatoes and butter over moderate heat, stirring from time to time so that the potatoes do not stick. Season with salt and pepper. When the potatoes are cooked, transfer them to a large shallow baking dish. Sprinkle with cheese, and break eggs over the potatoes and cheese, leaving a little space between each egg. Cover with cream. Sprinkle with salt and pepper. Brown in a hot (425° F or Gas No. 7) oven until the whites have set and the yolks are soft.

WINKLE OMELETTE

1 pt (2 cupfuls) winkles
6-8 eggs
1 oz butter
drop anchovy essence
pinch cayenne pepper
1 bay leaf
salt and pepper

FOR GARNISH
1 dessertspoon parsley — finely chopped

Poach winkles in boiling salted water with a bay leaf for 3 minutes. Remove from their shells. Lightly beat eggs with anchovy essence and cayenne pepper. Heat butter in omelette pan and when foaming pour in egg mixture. When nearly set but still a little runny add the winkles and fold in two. Serve immediately, sprinkled with finely chopped parsley.

Elizabeth H. O'Brien

COLD EGG MOUSSE

4 hard-boiled eggs
1 teaspoon worcester sauce
1 teaspoon bottled barbecue sauce
½ pt yoghourt or cream
1 teaspoon anchovy essence
½ pt aspic
pepper and paprika

Take yolks from hard-boiled eggs and sieve them. Add worcester and barbecue sauces, together with anchovy essence. Season to taste with pepper and paprika, but no salt. Mix half of the aspic with the egg yolks and let it set to the consistency of raw egg white. Then add the yoghourt or well whipped cream and the finely chopped egg whites. Mix all with an egg beater, place in a pyrex dish and let it get thoroughly cold. When set chop remaining aspic and put it on top of each portion ready to serve. Each portion should be served on a lettuce leaf.

Gwendolene Hirst

COLD CURRIED EGGS

8 *hard-boiled eggs*
5 *tablespoons double cream*
1 *tablespoon good curry powder*
salt and pepper

FOR GARNISH
4 *tomatoes — sliced*

Shell eggs, and cut lengthwise. Remove yolks and mash well. Combine cream with curry powder, add egg yolks and season. Fill egg whites with the mixture. Skin tomatoes and cut into thickish slices. Serve the eggs garnished with the tomato slices.

GREENFORT EGGS

4 hard-boiled eggs
1 small tin pâté — about $\frac{1}{4}$ lb
$\frac{3}{4}$ pt jellied stock
2-3 tablespoons cream
dash of brandy
1 teaspoon parsley — freshly chopped
1 teaspoon chives — freshly chopped
sprig tarragon — freshly chopped
few drops tabasco sauce
salt and pepper

Put pâté, eggs, $\frac{1}{4}$ pt of stock, cream and brandy into liquidiser and blend. Add seasoning and tabasco sauce. Spread mixture about $\frac{3}{4}$ inch to 1 inch deep in a flan or similar dish, or individual ramekins. Cover with even layer of jellied stock. Chill well. Just before serving, sprinkle fairly thickly with freshly chopped herbs. Serve with hot toast.

St Clerans, Galway

ST CLERANS EGGS
MADGE CREAGH'S RECIPE

8 *hard-boiled eggs*
1 *oz butter*
2 *tablespoons salad oil*
2 *oz onion — finely chopped*
6 *oz mushrooms — finely chopped*
1 *pt mornay sauce*
  (made with 2 oz butter, 2 oz flour,
  1 pt milk, 3 oz grated cheese)
16 *slices tomato*
1 *tablespoon parsley — chopped*
1 *tablespoon French mustard*
2 *cloves garlic — crushed*
3 *tablespoons cheese — grated*
salt and pepper

Heat oil and butter and sauté onion until soft and transparent. Add mushrooms, cook for a few minutes, then add parsley, mustard, garlic and seasoning. Cut eggs lengthways, remove yolks, mash them and add to the mixture. Fill into whites, arrange on an ovenproof dish on top of slices of tomato. Coat with sauce, sprinkle with cheese and brown in a hot oven.

Mrs John Huston

LOBSTER SOUFFLÉ

1 *lobster (live)*
2 *oz flour*
2 *oz butter*
¾ *pt milk*
½ *glass white wine*
4 *eggs*
1 *tablespoon brandy*
salt and pepper

COURT BOUILLON
3 *pt water*
1 *glass dry white wine*
1 *dessertspoon red wine vinegar*
1 *carrot*
1 *leek*
2 *onions*
4 *sprigs parsley*
4 *cloves*
salt and pepper

Combine ingredients of court bouillon, bring to the boil and simmer for 20 minutes. Plunge lobster into boiling court bouillon, return to boil and simmer for a further 20 minutes. Drain lobster, split and remove all flesh. Mince. Make a sauce with butter, flour and milk. Add white wine and lobster meat. Beat egg yolks well and add to the mixture. Season well, add brandy, and fold in stiffly beaten egg whites. Pour mixture into buttered ovenproof soufflé dish. Cook in fairly hot oven (400° F or Gas No. 6) for 25–30 minutes until golden brown and well risen.

Agnes Beresford - ASL

FILLETS OF SALMON GLENVEAGH
NELLIE GALLAGHER'S RECIPE

4-6 salmon cutlets
2 oz butter
juice 1 lemon
½ pt fish stock
4-6 haddock quenelles (see page 76)

FOR GARNISH
few cubes cucumber
tomato sauce (see page 199)

Poach the salmon cutlets in the oven in butter, lemon juice and fish stock, for about 15 minutes, according to size of cutlets. Make haddock quenelles and poach. Place one quenelle on each cutlet. Decorate with cubes of cucumber which have been cooked in a little butter until tender and pour round the cutlets a pale-coloured tomato sauce.

Henry P. McIlhenny

SALMON PIE
ANN SMITH'S RECIPE

$2\frac{1}{2}$ lb fresh salmon
2 oz parmesan cheese — grated
2 pt milk
$\frac{1}{2}$ clove garlic — crushed
2 oz flour
2 oz butter
salt and pepper

Poach the salmon for 15 minutes in the milk. Flake the salmon into a bowl and add most of grated cheese and crushed garlic. Combine the butter and flour in saucepan and make a white sauce with 1 pt of the milk used for poaching the fish. Add the white sauce to the fish until just moist. Add salt and pepper to taste. Place in greased ovenproof dish and sprinkle with the remaining grated cheese. Bake in oven for $\frac{1}{2}$ hour at 350° F or Gas No. 4.

Miranda Iveagh

SALMON FISH CAKES

½ lb fresh salmon — cooked and flaked
½ lb potatoes — freshly cooked and sieved
salt
peppercorns — freshly ground
2 oz butter
2 eggs — beaten
breadcrumbs
clarified butter for frying

Blend salmon well with potatoes. Season to taste with salt and pepper. Melt the butter and add it to the mixture, binding it with a beaten egg. Roll to 1½ inch thick and cut in desired shapes. Dip cakes into the other beaten egg and breadcrumbs, shaking off any surplus. Fry on both sides until golden brown.

SOMERTON SALMON STEAKS

4 $\frac{1}{2}$ lb salmon steaks
$\frac{1}{2}$ lb soft brown sugar
peppercorns — freshly ground
1 teaspoon mixed spice

Cover both sides of salmon steaks with mixture of brown sugar, pepper and mixed spice. Leave on a dish for 1 hour. Grill under very hot grill for 4 minutes each side.

Betsy Caroline Laidlaw

SKATE WITH BLACK BUTTER

4 *skate (ray) wings*
3 *tablespoons white vinegar*
salt
6 *peppercorns*

BLACK BUTTER
$\frac{1}{4}$ *lb butter*
1 *dessertspoon capers*
1 *teaspoon white wine vinegar*
1 *dessertspoon parsley — chopped*

Place skate wings in a saucepan with enough water to cover, with vinegar, salt and peppercorns. Bring to boiling point and simmer very gently for 8 minutes. Drain and remove skin and place on a heated dish. Make black butter by heating butter over low heat until dark brown but not burnt, then add vinegar, chopped parsley and capers. Pour immediately into a sauceboat, and serve.

SEAFIELD MACKEREL

4 medium-sized mackerel
1 oz butter
salt and pepper
½ pt béchamel sauce
   (made with ¾ oz butter, ¾ oz flour, ½ pt milk)
1 teaspoon horseradish
1 tablespoon powdered mustard
1 oz parmesan or cheddar cheese — grated

FOR GARNISH
fennel or parsley — chopped
1 lemon — quartered

Cook mackerel in covered frying pan with butter and seasoning until tender. Fillet the fish and arrange in shallow fireproof dish. Cover with béchamel sauce, well flavoured with mustard and horseradish. Sprinkle the fish with grated cheese and brown under hot grill. Serve with chopped fennel or parsley and lemon quarters.

Betty Tronley-Clarke

SNAFFLES,
47, LOWER LEESON STREET,
DUBLIN 2.
DUBLIN 60790

FILLETS OF TURBOT IN PUFF PASTRY

4 *fillets of turbot*
½ *lb puff pastry*
1 *small onion — finely chopped*
1 *tablespoon parsley — chopped*
¼ *lb mushrooms — chopped*
1 *oz butter*
4 *tablespoons dry white wine*
1 *egg yolk — beaten*
salt and pepper

Cook mushrooms, onion and parsley in butter and wine until soft. Roll out pastry into thin rectangles for each fillet. Place mushroom mixture on each sheet of pastry together with fish fillet, season, cover with pastry and press edges together with a fork. Paint pastry with beaten egg yolk. Cook in hot oven (425° F, Gas No. 7) for 15 minutes until pastry is golden brown. Serve with hollandaise sauce *(see page 195)*.

Glenarm Castle, Antrim

JELLIED EELS

2 lb eels — cleaned and skinned
2 medium-sized onions
1 bay leaf
1 tablespoon wine vinegar
2 oz leaf gelatine
2 sprigs parsley
2 pt cold water
whites and shells of 2 eggs
salt and pepper

Put eels into saucepan with all ingredients except egg whites and shells and gelatine. Simmer gently until eels are tender. Take out the fish, cut into pieces and remove the bones. Strain the liquid and return it to the pan, then add the crushed egg shells and lightly whisked whites of the eggs. Add gelatine and bring to the boil. Simmer for 2 minutes and strain again. Line a mould with the pieces of eel, add the jelly and leave to set.

SNAFFLES,
47, LOWER LEESON STREET,
DUBLIN 2.
DUBLIN 60790

STEAMED SOLE

4 fillets of Dover sole
1 lemon — quartered

Make sure skin is removed from both sides of the sole. Place it on a lightly buttered plate, and put it on a pan of boiling water. Turn another plate upside down over the fish. The fish will require no seasoning and will cook by steam. When cooked, serve with melted butter or hollandaise sauce *(see page 195)*.

SOLE IN EGGPLANT

2 *large eggplants (aubergines)*
4 *fillets of sole (or plaice)*
1 *small onion — finely chopped*
1 *oz butter*
milk for poaching
4 *oz cooked rice*
1 *dessertspoon tomato purée*
salt and pepper
1 *tablespoon cheese — grated*

SAUCE
$\frac{3}{4}$ *oz flour*
$\frac{3}{4}$ *oz butter*
$\frac{1}{2}$ *pt milk used for poaching fish*
1 *egg yolk*

Cut eggplants in half lengthwise. Salt each cut side and leave to drain for 1 hour. Fry in deep fat for a few minutes. Scoop out flesh, leaving shells intact. Cook onion in 1 oz butter. Poach fish fillets in milk. Make white sauce, using flour and butter, $\frac{1}{2}$ pt milk from fish and egg yolk. Mix together eggplant flesh, onion, rice, tomato purée, salt and pepper to taste. Fill eggplant shell with this mixture, placing a sole fillet on top of each one. Coat with white sauce. Sprinkle with grated cheese and brown under a grill.

75

HADDOCK QUENELLES
NELLIE GALLAGHER'S RECIPE

$\frac{1}{4}$ pt milk
2 oz fine stale breadcrumbs
1 egg — slightly beaten
2 tablespoons cream
$\frac{1}{2}$ lb raw haddock
1 oz butter
$\frac{1}{2}$ teaspoon salt
few grains pepper

Bind breadcrumbs and milk to paste. Meanwhile, force haddock through food mincer and work until smooth. Add it to the paste. Melt the butter and add it to paste, together with cream, egg, salt and pepper. Shape into small balls, or between teaspoons. Poach in boiling water or stock for 10 minutes.

Henry P. McIlhenny

COLD CURRIED FISH

$\frac{1}{2}$ lb spaghetti — cooked and cold
1-2 lb white fish — cooked and cold
1-2 pt white sauce — cold
1 (or more) tin shrimps
1 dessertspoon curry powder
chopped chives
1 teaspoon lemon juice
1 teaspoon redcurrant jelly or apricot jam

FOR GARNISH
parsley
paprika

Mix all ingredients gently together, sprinkle with parsley or paprika. Chill and serve.

SAVOURY HADDOCK
MAY A. CARROLL'S RECIPE

$\frac{1}{2}$ *lb thin streaky bacon rashers*
1 *lb haddock — filleted*

Cut the filleted haddock into 1-inch cubes. Wrap each one in streaky rasher and put on a skewer. Bake in oven until bacon is crisp. Serve with hot toast.

SNAFFLES,
47, LOWER LEESON STREET,
DUBLIN 2.
DUBLIN 60790

MARINATED WHITE FISH

1½ lb white fish (sole, plaice, etc.) — skinned and filleted
juice 3 lemons (or more, if necessary)
1 fresh chilli
1 teaspoon salt
black peppercorns — freshly ground

FOR GARNISH
1 tablespoon parsley or chives — finely chopped

Chop fish into 1-inch pieces. Place on smallish serving platter, sprinkle with salt and pepper and pour lemon juice over. Remove seeds from chilli and chop finely. Mix with fish and lemon juice. Make sure that the fish is just covered in lemon juice, and let it marinate for 4 hours. Turn occasionally. Serve sprinkled with parsley or chives and accompanied by hot brown toast.

79

COD WITH GARLIC

4 cod steaks
4 cloves garlic — crushed
4 oz butter
juice 2 lemons
salt and pepper

FOR GARNISH
1 dessertspoon parsley — finely chopped

Place cod steaks in ovenproof dish. Season with salt and pepper. Melt butter. Rub each steak with crushed garlic and pour melted butter and lemon juice over. Leave to marinate for at least 1 hour. Cook in a very hot oven (preheated to 450° F, Gas No. 9) for 8 minutes only. Decorate with parsley, and serve at once.

FISH SOUFFLÉ

$1\frac{1}{2}$ *lb smoked cod* or *haddock*
1 *pt milk*
1 *large onion — chopped finely*
5 *tablespoons olive oil*
2 *tablespoons breadcrumbs*
4 *eggs — beaten*
salt and pepper
1 *tablespoon parsley — chopped*

Poach fish in milk, drain and mince. Reserve milk. Cook chopped onion in olive oil until golden. Add breadcrumbs to reserved milk and boil, then add beaten eggs. Mix fish with onion, adding salt, pepper and parsley. Combine with the milk, breadcrumbs and beaten eggs, and bake in a well-buttered soufflé dish for about $1\frac{1}{2}$ hours in a slow to moderate oven (about 300° F, Gas No, 2).

Elizabeth Mount Charles

Lucan House, Dublin

KEDGEREE

1 lb smoked haddock — cooked
¼ lb butter
pinch cayenne pepper
pinch allspice
large pinch saffron
1 bay leaf
black peppercorns — freshly ground
8 oz rice
3 small onions — finely chopped
juice 1 lemon

Cook onions until golden brown in butter. Fry spices in same butter until dark brown. Add rice and sauté lightly. Add ¾ pt water, salt and bay leaf and simmer until rice is just cooked (12-15 minutes). Add fish and continue cooking until kedgeree is quite dry. Always cook very gently as it is easy to let rice burn or stick to bottom of pan. Discard bay leaf. Add lemon juice and serve piping hot with chutney — preferably homemade.

SNAFFLES,
47, LOWER LEESON STREET,
DUBLIN 2.
DUBLIN 60790

MARINATED KIPPERS

4 large Irish kippers on the bone
4 tablespoons olive oil
juice 1 lemon
1 tablespoon parsley — finely chopped

Skin and remove fillets from raw kippers. Lay on serving dish. Pour over olive oil and lemon juice. Leave to marinate for at least 1 hour. Sprinkle with parsley and serve with hot toast.

BARNADERG
LETTERFRACK
CO. GALWAY

SMOKED FISH MOUSSE

$\frac{1}{2}$ *lb smoked fish*
$\frac{1}{2}$ *pt milk*
$\frac{3}{4}$ *oz butter*
$\frac{3}{4}$ *oz flour*
2 *egg whites — stiffly beaten*
pinch cayenne pepper
pinch nutmeg
pinch turmeric
squeeze lemon juice

FOR GARNISH
chives or *parsley — finely chopped*

Cook the fish in the milk and drain. Make béchamel sauce using the same milk, butter and flour. Flake the fish finely and add to béchamel sauce. When cool, add a pinch of cayenne pepper, nutmeg, turmeric and the lemon juice. Fold in stiffly beaten egg whites. Chill. When well set, decorate with chives or parsley.

Elizabeth A. O'Brien

DRESSED CRAB

1 lb crab meat (2-3 crabs should yield this)
2 oz soft breadcrumbs
$\frac{1}{4}$ pt white sauce
$\frac{1}{2}$ tablespoon white wine vinegar
1 oz butter
2 tablespoons chutney
$\frac{1}{2}$ teaspoon mustard
salt and pepper

TOPPING
1 oz butter
1 oz breadcrumbs

Mix all ingredients together and pack into well scrubbed crab shells. Melt butter for topping, stir in crumbs and sprinkle on top. Heat through and brown top under grill.

G. Myrtle Allen

CLOSHEENS MARINIÈRE
QUEEN SCALLOPS

40 closheens
½ pt dry white wine
salt and pepper
½ onion — chopped finely
1 dessertspoon parsley — finely chopped
pinch fresh thyme
beurre manié (optional)

Place closheens in a saucepan with white wine, onion, parsley and thyme. Cook very quickly until closheens are just open. Remove the beards and black part and dip quickly in water to clean. Strain the wine sauce and put in cleaned closheens. Add salt and pepper to taste. If liked, beurre manié may be used to thicken the sauce. It is made by rubbing together equal quantities of butter and flour, and is sprinkled gradually into the hot liquid.

Mother Cusack

SCALLOP SOUFFLÉ

4 large scallops
¾ pt milk
1 ½ oz butter
2 oz flour
juice ½ lemon
6 eggs
salt
black peppercorns — freshly ground

Poach scallops in milk for 5 minutes. Make a white sauce with the butter, flour and the milk in which the scallops have been cooked. Add plenty of pepper and lemon juice. Cool and add 6 egg yolks, well beaten. Dice and add scallops. Fold in stiffly beaten egg whites. Pour into buttered soufflé dish and cook in hot oven (450° F or Gas No. 8) for 18 minutes, until well risen and golden brown.

Elizabeth A. O Brien

SCALLOPS WITH IRISH MIST

10 *scallops*
flour
2 *oz butter*
a little parsley — chopped
1 *shallot — minced*
$\frac{1}{4}$ *pt fresh cream*
1 *tablespoon Irish Mist Liqueur*
2 *egg yolks — beaten*
salt and pepper

Roll scallops in flour and sauté in half the butter for 3 minutes, then add cream, shallot and parsley and the Irish Mist liqueur. Season with salt and pepper. Allow to cook for a further 3 minutes. Take scallops from saucepan and place them in 4 empty scallop shells. Reduce sauce to half by boiling, add rest of butter and the egg yolks. Whisk together over a gentle heat until thickened but not boiling, and pour the sauce over the scallops. Place under very hot grill or salamander, glaze, and serve immediately.

Mrs John Williams

MUSSELS WITH TOMATO SAUCE

4 *dozen mussels*
3 *onions*
1 *large glass white wine* or *dry sherry*
1½ *lb tomatoes — skinned*
½ *cucumber — peeled*
1 *clove garlic*
lemon juice
salt and pepper
pinch cayenne pepper
olive oil (optional)

FOR GARNISH
parsley — chopped

Wash the mussels well and remove beards. Put into pan with 1 roughly chopped onion, enough water just to cover them, and wine (more wine may be used if you wish), salt and pepper. Cover and simmer until mussels open. Take mussels out and discard the topshell of each. Place mussels on a large platter and leave to cool. Blend tomatoes, cucumber and garlic in liquidiser. Add the remaining onions carefully in quarters and stop when the taste is to your palate. Pour mixture into a bowl, add lemon juice, salt, pepper and cayenne. A little olive oil and/or strained cooking liquid can be stirred in if desired. The sauce should be fairly thick. Spoon onto the mussels, scatter with chopped parsley and serve with brown bread and butter or French bread to mop up the sauce.

April Agnew Somerville

90

FILLETS OF CHICKEN WITH CUCUMBER
NELLIE GALLAGHER'S RECIPE

2 chicken breasts
2 oz butter
12 small whole onions
1 lb small mushrooms
2 oz flour
$\frac{1}{2}$ pt stock
$\frac{1}{4}$ pt double cream
4 oz bacon — diced
1 large cucumber — peeled and diced
1 glass madeira
parsley — chopped

Melt butter in a frying pan and add chicken. Cook for 10-15 minutes, remove chicken and keep hot in covered dish. Fry onion and mushrooms in frying pan until tender. Sprinkle with flour and gradually blend in the stock and cream. In a separate pan cook bacon and cucumber and add to sauce. Add madeira and cook slowly for 5 minutes. Arrange chicken on a serving platter and pour sauce over. Sprinkle with chopped parsley. Serve with boiled rice with grated carrot added.

Henry P. McIlhenny

CHICKEN AU GRATIN

1 *chicken (about 3 lb)*
1 *onion — chopped*
1 *teaspoon mixed herbs*
salt and ground black pepper
6 *stalks celery*
3 *oz butter*
2 *tablespoons tomato concentrate*
2 *carrots*
1 *small red pepper*
1 *small green pepper*
1 *teaspoon parsley — chopped*
2 *tablespoons parmesan cheese — grated*

Divide chicken into 8 pieces and remove skin. Put into saucepan with butter, onion, salt and black pepper, and cook until chicken is lightly golden. Add tomato concentrate, $\frac{1}{2}$ pt water, the carrots, celery and peppers cut into fine strips, the parsley and mixed herbs. Simmer for 1 hour. Place in serving dish and top with grated parmesan cheese. Serve with rice and green salad.

Donna Maria d'Ardia Caracciolo

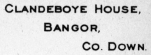

CLANDEBOYE CHICKEN

1 *chicken (about 3 lb) — freshly roasted*
$\frac{1}{2}$ *pt cream — stiffly whipped*
1 *teaspoon made English mustard*
2 *tablespoons worcester sauce*
salt and pepper
boiled rice
1 *teaspoon curry powder*
chutney

Joint chicken and arrange in a fireproof dish. Add mustard, salt and pepper, worcester sauce to cream. Pour over chicken and cook in hot oven until heated through. Serve with boiled rice flavoured with a teaspoon of curry powder and a little chutney.

Lindy Dufferin and Ava

Bermingham House, Tuam

BERMINGHAM CHICKEN

1 lb fresh spinach
2 oz butter
2 large slices cooked ham
4 uncooked chicken breasts — skinned
$\frac{1}{2}$ pt cheese sauce
   (made from $\frac{3}{4}$ oz butter, $\frac{3}{4}$ oz flour, $\frac{1}{2}$ pt milk,
    2 tablespoons grated cheese, salt and pepper)
pepper to taste
butter for cooking

Cook spinach in butter and pepper for a few minutes — no salt as it makes the spinach tough. Chop the spinach and place in a fireproof dish. Put slices of cooked ham and the chicken breasts on top and cover with cheese sauce. Cook in a moderate oven (350° F, Gas No. 4) for 35 minutes until golden brown.

Mother Cusack

WICKLOW CHICKEN

1 *boiling chicken* (3-4 *lb*)
1 *lb sausage meat*
2 *eggs*
1 *pt béchamel sauce*
  (*made with 2 oz butter, 2 oz flour, 1 pt milk*)
2 *onions — chopped*
parsley — chopped
6 *oz white breadcrumbs*
1 *teaspoon mixed herbs*
1 *tablespoon worcester sauce*
salt and pepper

Boil chicken until tender. Bone the chicken, discard the skin and mince the flesh. Chop the onions and add these and minced chicken to all the other ingredients. Mix until creamy and thoroughly blended. Turn into well greased baking case and bake in moderate to hot oven (350-400° F, Gas No. 4-5) for 1 hour or until free from sides of case. This can be eaten hot or cold, with green salad.

Donna Maria d'Ardia Caracciolo

CHICKEN VERMOUTH

1 *large roasting chicken* $(4\text{-}4\frac{1}{2}\,lb)$
2 *sprigs fresh tarragon*
$\frac{1}{2}$ *pt dry vermouth*
$\frac{1}{4}$ *pt cream*
salt and pepper
butter for roasting

Butter chicken inside and out and put tarragon inside, seasoning well. Pour $\frac{1}{4}$ pt dry vermouth over the bird, and roast in a hot oven until cooked brown and crispy, basting occasionally. Place chicken on a warm dish. Pour off any fat in the pan and into the residue put the remaining vermouth, the cream and a little water. Season very lightly, boil and allow to reduce by one third. Carve the chicken and pour the sauce over.

Betty Gransley-Clarke

GRILLED CHICKEN JOINTS WITH FRESH TARRAGON

4 chicken joints
6 sprigs fresh tarragon leaves — chopped
juice 1 lemon — squeezed
1 tablespoon olive oil
2 oz butter
black peppercorns — freshly ground

Marinate chicken joints for at least 1 hour in mixture of lemon juice, olive oil, tarragon and black pepper. Turn joints 2 or 3 times. Melt the butter and pour it over the chicken and put under the grill. Baste with the marinade during cooking and turn once. About 15-20 minutes should be enough. Just before serving sprinkle with more chopped tarragon. Serve with all the juices.

MOUNTJULIET,
THOMASTOWN,
Co. KILKENNY.

TARRAGON CHICKEN

1 *chicken (about* 3½ *lb)*
bunch fresh tarragon
4 oz butter
½ pt cream
½ chicken stock cube
black peppercorns — freshly ground
salt

Stuff chicken with tarragon. Add salt and pepper to taste. Sauté gently in butter in thick-bottomed saucepan until golden on all sides. Cover and simmer until tender. Take chicken from pan and remove tarragon. Add cream, ½ chicken stock cube to pan juices and simmer until sauce is smooth, but not too thick. Strain sauce over chicken and serve.

SLANE CHICKEN

4 chicken breasts — boned
¼ lb butter
1 tablespoon mustard powder
¼ pt tomato sauce
2 tablespoons consommé or good stock
2 tablespoons dry white wine
small glass brandy
small glass dry port or madeira
salt and pepper

Season boned chicken breasts with salt and fry lightly in butter. Mix together a little melted butter, mustard powder, tomato sauce and consommé (or stock). Add this to the juice from the fried chicken. Season, and add the dry white wine. Replace the chicken breasts in the sauce and simmer gently until tender (about 20 minutes). Just before serving, add the brandy and port or madeira. Serve with rice.

Elizabeth Mount Charles

CHEESEY CHICKEN

1 *roasting chicken*
  (about 3-4 lb, not frozen) — jointed and skinned
2 *oz butter*
3 *oz cheese — grated*
3 *oz breadcrumbs — browned*

Melt butter, mix cheese and breadcrumbs, dip chicken first in melted butter then in crumbs and cheese. Lay in shallow fireproof dish and pour over any remaining crumbs and butter. Bake, uncovered, in bottom of hot oven (400° F or Gas No. 6) for 1 hour. This can be prepared a day before it is needed, or can be prepared and put — uncooked — in the freezer.

Suzanne Mahon

PHEASANT AUX CHOUX

1 *cabbage — shredded*
1 *pheasant*
2 *onions*
2 *carrots*
2 *leeks*
3 *bacon rashers*
6 *peppercorns*
1 *bouquet garni*
2 *tablespoons port*

Blanch cabbage (put into cold water and bring to the boil). Strain immediately. Line casserole with cabbage and rest of vegetables. Put in the pheasant with bacon tied across breast and one onion inside. Add seasoning and port. Cover with water and simmer for 1½ hours. Strain and arrange pheasant on a bed of cabbage on a serving dish surrounded by the other vegetables.

Jessica Rathdonnell

PIGEON WITH RAISINS

2-3 oz raisins — stoned
4 plump wild pigeons
4-6 oz streaky bacon rashers
1 $\frac{1}{2}$ oz butter
$\frac{1}{2}$-$\frac{3}{4}$ pt brown jellied stock
16 small onions or 4 medium onions — diced
pepper to taste
castor sugar
cornflour for thickening (optional)

Soak the raisins in hot water until plump and soft. Split the pigeons in two and trim away the breast bone with scissors. Cut rashers into short strips and blanch (put into cold water and bring to the boil). Fry the bacon strips in butter for 2 or 3 minutes, then take them out and put in the pigeons which should be browned slowly on the skin side only. Take out the pigeon halves and pack them into a casserole with the bacon. Season well with pepper and pour over the stock barely to cover. Bring to the boil and cover tightly to cook for 1-1 $\frac{1}{2}$ hours or until done in the oven at 325° F or Gas No. 3. Meanwhile peel the onions and brown them in a pan giving them a dusting of castor sugar. Add them to the casserole after the first $\frac{1}{2}$ hour. Drain the raisins and add them to the casserole 15 minutes before serving. At the end of the cooking time the gravy should be well reduced (brown and sticky). If necessary, thicken with a little cornflour. Serve with purée of potatoes.

Phoenix Lodge, Dublin

PHEASANTS' BREASTS IN PUFF PASTRY WITH GRAPES AND BRANDY SAUCE

4 pheasants' breasts — skinned
½ lb puff pastry
20 grapes — skinned and stoned
2 egg yolks — beaten

Roll 4 lots of pastry to the thickness of a penny. Place a pheasant breast on each piece of pastry. Lay 5 grapes on top of each pheasant breast. Fold over pastry and seal the edges with a fork. Brush with egg yolks. Cook in hot oven (425° F or Gas No. 7) for 15-20 minutes until pastry is cooked. Serve with brandy sauce *(see page 209).*

PHEASANT CASSEROLE

For each pheasant
2 oz swiss truffled pâté
½ pt strong stock and madeira in equal quantities
   or *to taste*
3 bacon rashers — diced
1 dessertspoon brandy
1 tablespoon almonds — chopped
rock salt
ground pepper

FOR GARNISH
parsley — chopped

Roast pheasant sufficiently to be able to remove flesh from bones. (Breast can be removed in large pieces and the legs left whole.) Put meat in casserole, cover with slices of pâté and throw in almonds. Pour in stock and madeira and add bacon. Simmer in oven until cooked. Shortly before serving, add brandy and a little more madeira, plus rock salt and ground pepper to taste. Sprinkle with chopped parsley.

GAME PIE
MAY A. CARROLL'S RECIPE

pie crust — to cover pie dish
1 pheasant — boned and chopped in small pieces
½ hare or rabbit — boned and chopped in small pieces
2 lb calves' liver — cut into 1-inch squares
1 lb lean bacon — cut into 1-inch squares
1 oz butter
1 teaspoon allspice
2 tablespoons parsley — chopped
1 shallot — chopped finely
1 truffle
1 clove garlic — crushed
1 teaspoon mixed fresh herbs
salt and pepper
½ glass brandy
aspic jelly (optional)

Fry shallot very gently until transparent and put in mortar with garlic and fresh herbs. Pound well and season lightly with salt and pepper. Heat prepared meats in a little butter, but do not brown. Season with black pepper and allspice. Lay some of the liver on the bottom of the dish, then a layer of game, alternating brown and white meat, ending up with a layer of liver. Put a truffle and ½ glass of brandy over the pie. Then cover the pie with the crust and seal the edges. Steam for 4 hours and when done and cold take off crust. Seal with clarified butter and keep in a cool place for 3 weeks before eating. If liked, the butter can be taken off and the whole covered with aspic jelly.

PARTRIDGE WITH RED CABBAGE

2 young partridges
salt
peppercorns — freshly ground
2 oz butter
1 dessertspoon onion — chopped

$1\frac{1}{2}$ lb red cabbage — coarsely shredded
1 teaspoon lemon juice
4 tablespoons stock or water
sprig parsley — chopped

FOR SWEET—SOUR FLAVOUR
2 apples — peeled and sliced
1 tablespoon brown sugar
3 tablespoons red wine — vinegar

Split partridge open through back and fix it flat with a skewer. Rub a little salt and pepper over all surfaces. Brown bird and onion in butter. Grease a large casserole. Put in half the shredded cabbage, sprinkle with salt and pepper and about half the lemon juice. Add the partridge and onion and the butter in which they were cooked. Cover with remaining shredded cabbage, add a little more salt and pepper, remaining lemon juice and stock or water. Cover the dish closely and cook for $1\frac{1}{2}$ hours at 345° F or Gas No. 4 for the first $\frac{1}{2}$ hour, and at 300° F or Gas No. 2 for the remaining 1 hour or until bird and cabbage are tender. Serve on a dish, with the partridge cut in half on a mound of the cabbage and some of the cooking liquor poured over. Sprinkle with parsley. Pork chops can also be cooked in this way, but the cooking time is shorter.

If a sweet-sour flavour is preferred, the apples, brown sugar and red wine vinegar (mixed with the same quantity of water) can be tossed with the cabbage before putting into the casserole.

PIGEON SOUFFLÉ

6 oz pigeon — boned, cooked and minced
4 dessertspoons rice — cooked
2 oz butter
1 tablespoon good game stock
3 egg yolks
4 egg whites — stiffly beaten
salt and pepper

Pound prepared pigeon with butter, rice and stock, then season and rub through wire sieve or blend in liquidiser. Mix in egg yolks well and fold in egg whites. Place in buttered and floured soufflé dish on a dish of water. Cook in very moderate oven (300° F or Gas No. 2) for 1 hour. Serve with good game gravy.

SNIPE PUDDING

6 *snipe*
1 *medium onion — chopped*
1 *oz butter*
$\frac{1}{4}$ *lb mushrooms — chopped*
pinch fresh thyme
pinch fresh sage
2 *dessertspoons parsley — chopped*
2 *cloves garlic — crushed*
salt and pepper
$\frac{1}{4}$ *pt red wine*
$\frac{1}{4}$ *pt port*
juice 1 lemon
pinch nutmeg
trace cayenne pepper
8 *oz suet crust*
2 *truffles (optional)*

Cut the snipe in half. Remove gizzard and trail, put the trail on one side. Sauté onion in butter until golden brown, add mushrooms, herbs and seasoning. Add wine and port. Cook for 10 minutes. Add the trail and put all through sieve or put in liquidiser and blend. Season snipe with lemon juice, nutmeg and cayenne pepper. Line pudding basin with thin suet crust and put in the birds, with truffles if available. Pour the sauce over and put on a pastry lid. Steam for $1\frac{1}{2}$ hours.

RABBIT RABBLE

1 *large rabbit — jointed*
$\frac{1}{4}$ *lb fat bacon — cubed*
English mustard
$\frac{1}{2}$ *pt sour cream*
salt

Spread jointed rabbit with lots of mustard. Fry small cubes bacon and put in casserole. Fry jointed rabbit. Place in the casserole and cook at 400° F or Gas No. 6 for 35-40 minutes until tender. Transfer rabbit to a heated platter. Add sour cream to casserole and heat without boiling, scraping the juices that adhere to the pan. Season. Serve with steamed potatoes.

Mother Cusach

SPICED VENISON

3 oz rock salt
½ oz saltpetre
5 lb haunch venison — boned
1 teaspoon ginger — ground
1 teaspoon mace
1 teaspoon cloves — ground
¼ oz allspice — powdered
½ oz black pepper
3 oz brown sugar
1 carrot
2 sticks celery
1 onion

Mix ½ rock salt and saltpetre, rub well into boned meat. Put venison in earthenware dish for 24 hours. Mix spices well and rub into venison. Put venison back into its dish, sprinkle with mixture of salt and sugar. Turn it every day for 5 days. A liquid will form as the meat pickles, and it should be basted each day with this. After 5 days, wash meat well in cold water, roll it and tie securely. Cover with cold water and bring it slowly to the boil. Add the vegetables and simmer very gently for 3 hours until meat is tender. Let meat cool in its own liquid. Then remove it and press with a weight.

GLASLOUGH HARE

1 *hare (well hung, keeping blood) — skinned and jointed*
1 *bottle red wine*
$\frac{1}{4}$ *pt olive oil*
3 *onions — chopped*
3 *cloves garlic*
12 *juniper berries — crushed*
2 *bay leaves*
sprig thyme
$\frac{1}{2}$ *bottle port*
salt and pepper

Put the jointed hare in a large flat roasting dish. Reserve the blood. Add wine, olive oil, onions, salt, pepper, garlic, juniper berries, bay leaves and thyme and marinate for at least 24 hours, turning pieces of hare several times. Take hare out, dry, roll in seasoned flour and fry quickly in oil. Put in casserole with strained juices of the marinade. Cook at 200° F or Gas No. $\frac{1}{2}$ for 2 hours. Add port and cook for another hour until tender. Add the blood 10 minutes before serving. Make sure not to boil the blood as it will curdle.

Helen Leslie

Farmleigh, Castleknock, Dublin

IRISH BEEF CASSEROLE

$1\frac{1}{2}$ lb stewing steak — cubed
1 oz dripping
1 oz flour
1 clove garlic
$\frac{1}{2}$ pt stock
1 level teaspoon dry mustard
$\frac{1}{2}$ a green pepper — sliced
4 oz mushrooms
1 large onion — sliced
$\frac{1}{2}$ pt Guinness
1 bouquet garni

Heat dripping in a pan and brown the cubed meat. Stir in the flour. Add Guinness, stock, garlic, bouquet garni and mustard. Bring slowly to the boil. Pour into ovenproof casserole and cook for $2\frac{1}{2}$ hours at 300° F or Gas No. 2. Add sliced pepper, sliced onion and mushrooms. Cook for a further $\frac{1}{2}$ hour and check seasoning.

Miranda Iveagh

STEAK IRISH MIST

4 sirloin steaks
$\frac{1}{4}$ *pt thick cream*
2 tablespoons Irish Mist Liqueur
2 oz butter
salt
peppercorns — freshly ground

FOR GARNISH
watercress

Remove sirloin steaks from bone, season well with salt and pepper. Heat pan, and when very hot add a knob of butter. When butter bubbles add steaks and cook for 4 minutes (or longer if desired) on either side. Remove to warm platter. Add cream to juices in pan, then add Irish Mist liqueur, stir and pour over steaks. Serve garnished with watercress.

Mrs John Williams

SNAFFLES,
47, LOWER LEESON STREET,
DUBLIN 2.
DUBLIN 60790

BEEF STEW WITH BEER

1 ½ *lb round steak — cut in 1-inch squares*
4 *oz good dripping or lard*
1 *tablespoon flour*
4 *large onions — chopped coarsely*
1 *teaspoon mixed herbs*
sprig parsley
½ *pt lager*
1 *beef stock cube*
1 *large slice bread*
2 *tablespoons French mustard*
black peppercorns — freshly ground

Roll meat in flour. Fry in dripping until golden brown. Remove to casserole. Fry onions lightly and add to meat in casserole. Add parsley, herbs, lager, stock cube and black pepper. Spread bread on both sides with mustard and place on top. Cover casserole and cook at 275° F or Gas No. 1 for 4 hours.

Lisnavagh.

Rathvilly

Ireland.

MEAT LOAF

1 *lb meat — minced*
1 *lb breadcrumbs*
1 *large onion — chopped*
1 *tablespoon chutney*
1 *tablespoon parsley — chopped*
1 *tablespoon mint — chopped*
1 *tablespoon thyme — chopped*
salt and pepper
½ *lb shortcrust pastry*

Mix together meat, breadcrumbs, onion and herbs. Add egg, chutney, salt and pepper. Roll out pastry into a square. Put meat mixture down the centre and trim pastry to come half way over the meat. Damp and cut strips of pastry and lay criss-cross along the top. Bake in moderate oven (350° F or Gas No. 4) for ½ hour.

Jessica Rathdonnell

GAELIC STEAK

4 fillet steaks (4-6 oz each)
2 oz butter
2 tablespoons shallots or green onions — finely chopped
$\frac{1}{4}$ lb mushrooms — sliced
$\frac{1}{2}$ pt double cream
$\frac{1}{4}$ pt Irish Whiskey
salt
black peppercorns — freshly ground

FOR GARNISH
1 tablespoon parsley — finely chopped

Melt the butter over medium heat in a large frying pan. Add steaks and sauté quickly, turning once. Time about 1$\frac{1}{2}$ minutes each side. Season with salt and pepper. Remove steaks to heatproof dish and keep warm. Add chopped shallots and mushrooms to frying pan, sauté until shallots tender and mushrooms lightly browned. Add cream and Irish whiskey. Cook over medium heat until sauce is reduced by half. Pour sauce over steaks, sprinkle with chopped parsley and serve at once.

Nicola O'Reilly

Nevara
21 Temple Gardens
Dublin 6

STEWED OX TAIL

2 small ox tails
2 onions
2 oz butter or olive oil
$1\frac{1}{2}$ oz flour
$1\frac{1}{2}$ pt good stock
1 bouquet garni
cloves to taste
mace to taste
juice $\frac{1}{2}$ lemon
salt and pepper

Wash tails, dry well and remove any superfluous fat. Cut into joints and divide the thick parts in half. Melt butter in saucepan. Fry the pieces of the tail until brown, then remove from pan. Slice onions and fry until light brown, add flour, mix well and cook until a good brown colour. Add stock, salt, pepper, bouquet garni, cloves and mace and bring to boiling point, stirring all the time. Add pieces of tail and simmer gently for approximately $2\frac{1}{2}$ - 3 hours. Remove meat and arrange on a heated serving dish. Add lemon juice to sauce, check seasoning, strain and pour over meat. Serve with croutons and cooked carrot and turnip.

Jerry Butt

LAMB WITH ROSEMARY

leg of lamb (4-5 lb)
garlic cloves — cut into slivers
olive oil
3 oz dried rosemary
glass sweet sherry
coarse cooking salt
black peppercorns — ground

Insert slivers of garlic into small gashes made all over the leg of lamb. Paint the joint with olive oil and rub with coarse cooking salt mixed with ground black pepper and about 3 oz rosemary. If any fresh or dried sprigs of rosemary are available, tie them to the outside of the joint. Place the joint in the oven at maximum temperature for 15 minutes, then reduce to moderate and cook for another 15 minutes per lb. When it is half done, baste regularly for the rest of the cooking time with the sweet sherry. Serve the strained juices as gravy and, where available, serve juniper berry conserve or red currant jelly on the side.

STUFFED SHOULDER OF CONNEMARA LAMB

1 *shoulder of lamb (about 3½ lb) — boned*
3 *oz rice — cooked*
2 *oz sultanas*
rind ½ *orange — coarsely chopped*
marjoram
1 *clove garlic — crushed*
1 *tablespoon flour*
2 *tablespoons oil*
1½ *lb potatoes — peeled and cut up*
¼ *pt stock*
6 *tomatoes*
salt and pepper

Mix rice, sultanas, orange rind, little marjoram, crushed garlic and seasoning together for stuffing. Spread on inner surface of meat, roll up and tie. Rub surface with flour. Calculate cooking time (15-20 minutes per lb) and put lamb in tin with oil and potatoes. Pour on stock and cover with foil. Roast at 350° F or Gas No. 4. Halfway through cooking time remove foil and baste. 25 minutes before end of cooking put in tomatoes. Boil remaining liquid in roasting tin and serve as gravy with tomatoes round joint and potatoes separately.

Philippa Dunalley

MARINATED LEG OF LAMB

leg of lamb (4-4½ lb)
3 tablespoons French dressing
1 clove garlic — crushed
½ teaspoon sage
½ teaspoon thyme
2 teaspoons sugar
butter and oil for cooking

Prick leg of lamb all over with carving fork and pour on French dressing. Rub over with crushed garlic, and then sprinkle with sage and thyme. Cover and leave to marinate overnight, spooning juice over as often as possible. Cook in a moderate oven (about 350° F or Gas No. 4) with oil and butter for 2 hours, sprinkle over with sugar and cook for a further ½ hour. Baste frequently.

Sybil Connelly

Flesk Castle, Kerry

LOIN OF LAMB IN PUFF PASTRY

4 loin chops — boned, rolled and skinned
$\frac{1}{2}$ lb puff pastry
2 egg yolks — well beaten

HERB BUTTER
$\frac{1}{4}$ lb butter
4 rosemary leaves — chopped
2 cloves garlic — crushed
black peppercorns — freshly ground
1 dessertspoon parsley — finely chopped

Roll pastry out into 4 rectangles. Place a lamb chop on pastry and spread on herb butter. Cover and seal pastry with a fork. Brush with beaten egg yolks and bake in hot oven (400° F or Gas No. 6) for 15 minutes, until the pastry is well puffed up and golden brown. Lamb should be pink and juicy.

GREY ABBEY.
NEWTOWNARDS,
CO. DOWN.

PORK CHOP IN ORANGE MAYONNAISE

4 *loin pork chops*
breadcrumbs
½ *pt mayonnaise mixed with 1 tablespoon concentrated orange juice*
   and seasoned with crushed garlic
butter for frying

Prepare pork chops by removing bone and excess fat. Place on board and beat until paper-thin. Dip in mayonnaise/orange mixture, coat in breadcrumbs and fry quickly in butter until golden brown. Drain and serve at once with a tossed green salad.

Daphne Montgomery

PORK CASSEROLE

top half of leg of pork — skinned
1 oz butter
2 shallots — chopped
milk to cover joint
pinch nutmeg or mace

Grease saucepan (size to fit meat) with a little butter. Brown joint all over and remove from pan. Sweat shallots in fat until golden brown. Remove fat and replace joint and shallots in saucepan. Season with salt, pepper, nutmeg or mace. Add enough milk to cover and bring to boil. Place immediately in moderate oven to keep milk very gently simmering until meat is cooked. Remove meat, strain off fat, and thicken the milk mixture with beurre manié *(see page 87)* and use as gravy, seasoning to taste.

ROAST PORK WITH HERBS

loin of pork (at least 3 lb)
3 teaspoons lemon rind — grated
handful parsley — chopped
1 teaspoon basil — chopped
2 cloves garlic — crushed
3 level teaspoons onion — finely chopped
3 tablespoons olive oil
½ glass red wine or sherry

The day before the joint is to be served, all the herbs, the basil, parsley, garlic, onion and lemon rind should be mixed thoroughly together and rubbed well into the skin of the joint after it has been thoroughly scored with a sharp knife. The joint should then be wrapped up in kitchen foil and placed in the refrigerator for the night.

Remove the joint from the fridge 1 hour before starting to cook and brush the skin well with olive oil before roasting. Put the meat on a rack in a 375°-400° F or Gas No. 5-6 oven and allow ½ hour per lb for cooking. When cooked, skim off the excess fat from the gravy and add a little red wine or sherry. Serve with broad beans and mashed potatoes, or seasonal vegetables to choice.

Maureen Cooper

DUBLIN CODDLE

2 *lb green bacon*
½ *lb pork sausages*
2 *large onions*
4 *large potatoes*
1 *bouquet garni*
salt and pepper

FOR GARNISH
chopped parsley

Soak bacon in water overnight. Cut into cubes and put into stew pan and cover with water. Bring slowly to the boil, skim and simmer for 1 hour. Peel and slice the potatoes and onions. Cut sausages into chunks and, together with the potatoes, onions, salt and pepper and bouquet garni, add to the bacon and simmer for ½ hour. Sprinkle on chopped parsley before serving.

Miranda Iveagh

GLIN CASTLE
CO. LIMERICK
IRELAND.

BAKED LIMERICK HAM
NANCY ELLIS'S RECIPE

1 *ham (12 lb)*
$\frac{1}{2}$ *glass brandy*
$\frac{1}{2}$ *pt beer*
$\frac{1}{2}$ *lb brown sugar*
4 *oz butter*
$\frac{1}{4}$ *oz cloves*

Bake ham for $4\frac{1}{2}$ hours in oven at 300° F or Gas No. 2. When cooked, remove the skin, and make a paste with the brandy, butter and sugar. Coat ham with the paste and stick in the cloves. Bake in the oven until a nice golden brown. Pour beer over ham. Serve hot or cold.

Olda Fitzgerald

PIGS' FEET WITH MUSTARD SAUCE

4 pigs' feet
½ pt cold mustard sauce (see page 207)
olive oil
fresh breadcrumbs
4 pt light stock or *water*

Simmer the pigs' feet in the stock or water for 3 hours until tender.
Remove bones, keeping the foot intact as much as possible. Dip each foot
in olive oil and breadcrumbs. Place on serving platter and cook in very
hot oven (450° F or Gas No. 8) until crisp and golden brown. Serve immediately with mustard sauce.

TONGUE WITH BERMINGHAM SAUCE

1 tongue — pickled
2 tablespoons white sugar
2 tablespoons butter
tabasco to taste
4-5 medium tomatoes — peeled
1 small onion
1 small cooked carrot — coarsely chopped
1 tablespoon fresh lemon juice
salt and pepper to taste
4 pt water

Cook pickled tongue slowly in water for 3-3 $\frac{1}{2}$ hours until skin comes off easily. Caramelise the sugar lightly with butter. Add tabasco to taste. Add vegetables and season. Cook *very* slowly until soft, and sieve. Add lemon juice. Serve hot or cold.

Mother Cusack

GLIN CASTLE
CO. LIMERICK
IRELAND.

PRESSED OX TONGUE
NANCY ELLIS'S RECIPE

1 *ox tongue — pickled*
6 *bay leaves*
sprig rosemary
1 *clove garlic*
1–3 *oz packet aspic jelly*

FOR GARNISH
4 *sprigs parsley*
1 *red pepper — sliced*

Soak the tongue in cold water for 2–3 hours. Drain, cover with fresh water, add bay leaves, rosemary and garlic and simmer for 4 hours until tender when pierced by a fork. Add aspic jelly to 1 pt cooking liquid. Skin tongue, place in a bowl and pour aspic over it. Leave to get cold and set. Decorate with parsley and red pepper. Serve thinly sliced on a bed of crisp lettuce.

Olda Fitzgerald

Bear Forest, Cork

CALVES' LIVER WITH MARROW

4 *medium slices calves' liver*
1 *marrowbone*
1 *lemon — cut in quarters*
2 *oz butter*
salt
black peppercorns — freshly ground

Poach marrowbone in salted simmering water for 8 minutes. Remove marrow from bone and leave in hot water off heat. Fry liver very gently in butter for about 2 minutes each side until still pink but cooked. Remove to heated platter, season with salt and freshly ground black pepper. Serve with slices of marrow on each piece of liver and a quarter of lemon.

CALVES' BRAINS IN PUFF PASTRY

2 sets calves' brains
2 tablespoons white wine vinegar
⅔ lb puff pastry
2 egg yolks — well beaten
1 teaspoon salt
½ pt egg and lemon sauce
or melted butter

Soak brains for at least 1 hour in cold water with 1 tablespoon of vinegar. Remove membrane and bloody tissue and put the cleaned brains in fresh cold water. Add the other tablespoon vinegar and the salt to a saucepan of simmering water. Add brains and simmer very gently for ½ hour. Drain well and dry. Roll out pastry into 4 rectangles. Place a half set of brains on each piece of pastry, cover and seal with a fork. Brush with egg yolks and cook in a hot oven (400° F or Gas No. 6) for 15-20 minutes until pastry is golden brown. Serve with egg and lemon sauce, or with melted butter.

SWEETBREAD AND CHICKEN SOUFFLÉ
NELLIE GALLAGHER'S RECIPE

$\frac{1}{2}$ *lb cooked white sweetbreads — diced*
$\frac{1}{2}$ *lb cooked chicken — diced*
1 *pt cream — whipped*
$\frac{1}{2}$ *pt aspic*
$\frac{1}{2}$ *lb peas — cooked*
4 *small tomatoes*
1 *truffle — chopped*
oil
vinegar
salt and pepper

Line a pipe mould with aspic and put on ice until set. Mix together rest of whipped aspic, sweetbreads, chicken and whipped cream. Season well. Pour onto mould. Leave to set in a cool place. When firm, turn out. Fill centre with peas and small skinned tomatoes scooped out and filled with chopped truffle mixed with oil and vinegar.

Henry P. McIlhenny

SWEETBREADS IN TOMATO SAUCE

1 *lb lambs' sweetbreads*
olive oil
1 *large Spanish onion — finely chopped*
1 *tablespoon tomato purée*
1 *glass sherry*
$\frac{1}{4}$ *pt strong stock*
2-3 *tablespoons sour cream*
1 *dessertspoon flour*
1 *dessertspoon paprika*
pinch cinnamon
salt and pepper

Leave sweetbreads to soak for several hours in water with dash of vinegar added. Drain and clean. Cover with fresh water and blanch, then leave between 2 plates with a weight on top until ready to use. Fry the chopped onion in oil until transparent. Add the sweetbreads and the flour and paprika, the tomato purée, the stock and the sherry. Stir occasionally to make it blend well, add salt and pepper and cinnamon to taste. Before serving add the sour cream and serve on a bed of rice.

April Agnew Somerville

TRIPE CASSEROLE

1½ lb tripe
4 onions — cut in very thin slices
¼ pt olive oil
4 shallots — peeled
2 cloves garlic — crushed
1 glass brandy
2 tablespoons tomato purée
¼ pt dry white wine
sprig thyme
2 teaspoons parsley — chopped
salt and pepper
1 tablespoon vinegar

Parboil tripe for a few minutes. Drain and rinse in cool water. Remove skin and scrape exterior. Soak 12 hours in cold water, changing water occasionally. Boil 2-3 hours in water flavoured with vinegar.

Cook onions in olive oil until soft and transparent. Boil shallots for 5 minutes, and drain well. Sauté sliced tripe in rest of oil until golden brown. Add onions and shallots. Add brandy and flame. Stir until flames subside. Add garlic, tomato purée, white wine, ¼ pt water, herbs and seasoning. Stir well and cook covered in casserole in moderate oven (350° F or Gas No. 4) for 1 hour.

SNAFFLES,
47, LOWER LEESON STREET,
DUBLIN 2.
DUBLIN 60790

CABBAGE STUFFED WITH HAM

1 medium-sized cabbage
½ lb soft white breadcrumbs
½ lb cooked ham — minced
½ lb bacon — finely diced
¼ pt milk
1 shallot — chopped
2 egg yolks — well beaten
2 tablespoons parsley, chives and tarragon
¾ pt stock
salt and pepper

Boil cabbage for 15 minutes and drain, spreading out leaves of core.
Prepare stuffing by putting bread and milk in bowl, mixing well and
pouring off any excess milk. Add ham, bacon and herbs and season well.
Add egg yolks. Put a little stuffing between each leaf and the rest in the
centre. Re-form cabbage and tie with string. Place cabbage in deep pan,
add stock and simmer gently covered for 3 hours.

RED CABBAGE

1 *small red cabbage (about 2 lb)*
1 *large onion — sliced*
2 *oz butter* or *dripping*
1 *oz flour*
2 *apples — peeled, cored and cut in chunks*
3 *tablespoons white* or *wine vinegar*
2 *teaspoons brown sugar*
3-4 *cloves (optional)*
3-4 *bay leaves (optional)*
salt

Wash and shred cabbage. Heat fat in fairly large saucepan and lightly fry onion. Add flour and cook for a minute or two, but do not brown. Add $\frac{1}{2}$ pt water, apples, vinegar, sugar, cloves, bay leaves, salt to taste and the cabbage. Simmer, stirring at intervals, until cabbage is tender (about $1\frac{1}{2}$-2 hours). There should be no liquid to throw away.

Castle Coole, Fermanagh

BROAD BEANS WITH CREAM AND TARRAGON

1 *lb young broad beans — shelled*
2 *oz butter*
2 *egg yolks*
4 *tablespoons double cream*
juice ½ lemon
2 *teaspoons fresh tarragon — chopped*
salt and pepper

Melt butter, add beans, cover and cook very gently until beans are tender (10-20 minutes). Season. The cooking time will depend on the age of the beans. Shake pan occasionally so that the beans do not stick. Beat egg yolks in cream, and add lemon juice and tarragon. Stir sauce into beans — do not boil, but just heat. (N.B. Only use tarragon if very fresh.)

BROAD BEANS AND BACON

1 *lb broad beans*
¾ *lb smoked back rashers — cut very thin*
1 *oz butter*
salt
black peppercorns — ground

Bring to the boil a pan of salted water, put in beans and cook for about 6 minutes until just tender, drain, and place in a dish with the butter and ground black pepper. Meanwhile grill or fry the bacon rashers, chop them up and stir through the beans. Serve immediately.

April Agnew Somerville

COS LETTUCE IN CHEESE SAUCE

4 cos lettuces
¼ pt chicken stock

CHEESE SAUCE
1 oz butter
1 oz flour
½ pt milk
1 ½ oz parmesan — grated
1 ½ oz gruyère — grated
salt and pepper
pinch cayenne peper

Blanch the lettuces in boiling salted water for 1 minute. Drain and put in a casserole dish with stock — do not cover. Cook in the oven for ½ hour (350° F or Gas No. 4). Meanwhile make the cheese sauce. Heat the butter, blend in flour, then milk. Continue cooking until mixture thickens and boils. Stir in cheese and reheat but do not allow to reboil. Season with salt, pepper and cayenne pepper. Take lettuces out and drain off stock, add some of the stock to the sauce and then pour over the lettuce and put back into the oven for 10 minutes.

April Agnew Somerville

GLIN CASTLE
CO. LIMERICK
IRELAND.

STUFFED VEGETABLE MARROW
NANCY ELLIS'S RECIPE

1 medium-sized vegetable marrow
$\frac{1}{2}$ lb ham — minced
$\frac{1}{2}$ lb lamb — minced
1 large onion — chopped
1 bay leaf — crushed finely
1 tablespoon sherry
2 oz butter

Cut marrow in half and remove all seeds and the skin. Place in baking dish and stuff with mixture of lamb, ham, onion, bay leaf, butter and sherry. Bake in the oven for 1 hour at 350° F or Gas No. 4. Serve with green salad.

Olda Fitzgerald

SPINACH IN CREAM

4 *lb fresh spinach*
$\frac{1}{4}$ *pt double cream*
3 *oz butter*
salt and pepper

Trim the large stems from the spinach and wash well, changing the water 3 times. Cook in covered saucepan with only the water that clings to the spinach, for about 7 minutes until tender. Drain very well, press out all water and force through a food mill. Reheat spinach in butter in saucepan and, just before serving, add cream and season. Heat well, but do not boil. Serve immediately on preheated vegetable dish.

STUFFED ONIONS

8 *large onions*
½ *lb mushrooms*
2 *oz butter*
2 *tablespoons parsley — chopped*
¼ *pt good chicken stock*
2 *cloves garlic — crushed*
salt and pepper

Peel onions and cut tops off. Boil for 5 minutes and drain very well. Chop onion tops and mushrooms. Sweat onions, mushrooms and garlic in butter until soft and transparent. Season and add parsley. Hollow out onions, leaving shell ½ inch thick. Fill with stuffing. Bake in oven dish with stock for ½ hour at 400° F or Gas No. 6 until cooked.

BRAISED LEEKS

$2\frac{1}{2}$ *lb leeks*
3 oz butter
$\frac{1}{4}$ *pt good chicken stock*
salt and pepper

Remove green part of leeks and wash remainder carefully. Place in covered casserole with butter, salt, pepper and stock. Cook in low oven (250-300° F or Gas No. 1-2) for 1 hour.

BAKED STUFFED POTATOES
NANCY ELLIS'S RECIPE

6 *medium-sized potatoes*
1 *tablespoon parsley — chopped*
1 *tablespoon butter*
2 *tablespoons chives — chopped*
2 *cloves garlic — crushed*
$\frac{1}{4}$ *lb strong cheese — grated*

Thoroughly wash potatoes and bake in oven at 300° F or Gas No. 2 for 1 hour. When potatoes are tender, remove the inside, keeping the shell separate. Mash the insides with garlic, parsley, butter and chives. Return mixture to the potato shells and sprinkle with grated cheese. Return to oven for 10 minutes until golden crispy brown. Good with cold meat or baked ham.

Olda Fitzgerald

AMBROSIA

4 large potatoes — peeled and diced
2 tablespoons good pork or bacon dripping
2 or 3 eggs — well beaten
salt and black pepper

Put dripping into heavy frying pan. Spread potato dice evenly over pan, pressing down into a thick layer. Sprinkle with salt and black pepper. Cover with a large plate or lid. Stand pan for 5 minutes over high heat, then lower heat and cook, undisturbed, until potato is tender (about 20-25 minutes). Increase heat to brown bottom of potato. Season beaten eggs, pour over potato, and cook 5 minutes more until eggs are set. Loosen all round with a palette knife and turn out whole on a hot dish. The eggs may be varied by adding grated cheese, chopped cooked bacon, mushrooms, etc.

Suzanne Mahon

POTATO SOUFFLÉ

6 medium-sized potatoes — peeled
4 oz butter
$\frac{1}{4}$ pt milk
3 egg yolks — whisked
4 egg whites — stiffly beaten
salt and pepper

Cook potatoes until tender. Heat milk. Drain and force potatoes through a food mill. Beat in butter and hot milk, season and cool. Add whisked egg yolks, beating well, to mixture. Fold in egg whites. Pour mixture into buttered soufflé dish and bake in an oven at 425°F or Gas No. 7 for 25 minutes until golden brown.

POTATO PANCAKES

2 potatoes — peeled
2 heaped tablespoons flour
1 teaspoon each salt and pepper
2 eggs
olive oil

Grate potatoes on medium grater. Mix flour, salt and pepper, and add to potatoes. Then add 2 eggs, broken in one at a time. Beat all together into a rough purée. Lightly cover bottom of frying pan with olive oil and heat. Put 1 teaspoon of the mixture into the hot oil for each pancake. Spread out quickly with a spoon into thin ragged shapes. Fry until crisp on both sides. Serve hot with cold beetroot slices.

Mountbatten of Burma

POTATO CAKES WITH SOUR CREAM

2 *lb potatoes*
1 *tablespoon sea salt*
black pepper
1 *tablespoon onion — grated*
2 *tablespoons flour*

FOR GARNISH
1 *jar Danish caviar*
$\frac{1}{2}$ *pt sour cream*
1 *tablespoon chives — chopped finely*

Boil potatoes until soft. Skin them and sieve. Add sea salt, black pepper, grated onion and flour. Mix well, roll out and cut into rounds $\frac{1}{4}$ inch thick. Cook on hot griddle or in iron pan with a smear of butter until the cakes are light brown on both sides. Serve hot with a tablespoon of sour cream and a teaspoon of caviar on each. Sprinkle with chopped chives.

Helen Leslie

SNAFFLES,
47, LOWER LEESON STREET,
DUBLIN 2.
DUBLIN 60790

MUSHROOM SALAD

¾ lb button mushrooms — sliced
1 tablespoon parsley or chives — finely chopped
3 cloves garlic — squeezed
8 tablespoons good olive oil
juice 2 lemons
salt and pepper

Put mushrooms into a salad bowl. Mix in the garlic, parsley or chives, oil and lemon juice. Season to taste. Marinate for at least 2 hours. The mushrooms will release some oil. Serve with hot toast.

RAINBOW SALAD

2 *green eating apples*
$\frac{1}{2}$ *head celery*
2 *large carrots — scraped*
2 *green peppers*
1 *cucumber*
1 *hard-boiled egg — chopped*
$\frac{1}{2}$ *pt mayonnaise*
1 *tablespoon parsley — finely chopped*
salt
black peppercorns — freshly ground

Cut all vegetables into small slices. Mix well with mayonnaise. Season with salt and black pepper to taste. Place in serving dish or salad bowl, sprinkle with chopped parsley and egg.

HAZELNUT SALAD

$\frac{1}{2}$ *lb French beans — cooked*
$\frac{1}{2}$ *lb haricot beans — cooked*
1 *stalk celery — chopped*
$\frac{1}{4}$ *lb roasted hazelnuts — chopped roughly*
vinaigrette dressing

Combine beans and celery in a salad bowl. Add nuts and mix well with vinaigrette dressing.

Hollywell Cottage, Cavan

SPINACH AND CARROT SALAD

1 *lb spinach*
1 *lb carrots — grated*
1 *head lettuce*
$\frac{1}{4}$ *pt mayonnaise*
juice 1 *lemon*
2 *hard-boiled eggs — chopped*

Wash spinach very well, changing water several times. Discard all stems and tear spinach into shreds. Trim, wash and break lettuce head into leaves. Mix carrots and spinach with mayonnaise and a little lemon juice. Line large salad bowl with 4 large lettuce leaves. Divide spinach mixture on each leaf. Sprinkle with chopped hard-boiled eggs.

IRISH MIST SOUFFLÉ

juice 1 *lemon*
1 *sweet geranium leaf*
2 *eggs*
2 *oz castor sugar*
1 *dessertspoon Irish Mist Liqueur*
1 *rounded teaspoon powdered gelatine*

Squeeze lemon and soak the geranium leaf in the juice. Beat egg yolks and sugar to a thick mousse, add the Irish Mist and beat again. Dissolve gelatine in one teaspoon of the lemon juice and two of water warmed slightly and add to mousse with the remaining lemon juice. Fold in stiffly beaten egg whites. Freeze inside scooped out lemons or in a soufflé dish for a few hours before serving.

G. Myrtle Allen

RUM SOUFFLÉ

3 *eggs*
2 *oz castor sugar*
$2\frac{1}{2}$ *leaves gelatine*
$\frac{1}{2}$ *pt cream*
2 *tablespoons rum*

Separate egg yolks from whites. Melt gelatine leaves in a little warm water. Whip egg whites and half whip the cream. Then beat yolks and sugar together for a few minutes and quickly add the melted gelatine. Add the cream and fold in whites of eggs. Add rum and chill for 3 hours before serving.

Mary Davies

APRICOT SOUFFLÉ

4 egg whites
2 tablespoons apricot jam

Whip the whites of egg stiffly and fold in the apricot jam. Put mixture into a soufflé dish, filling it nearly to the top. Stand the dish over a saucepan of boiling water, which you then remove from the heat, but keep warm for 1 hour or more. Serve with cream.

Diana Farnham

BAKED ORANGE SOUFFLÉ

6 eggs
1 lemon
3 oranges
6 oz icing sugar — sieved

Separate yolks from whites of eggs. Grate rind of lemon and oranges and squeeze juice. Put juice, rind, sugar and 5 egg yolks into basin and beat over a pan of hot water until thick and creamy. Remove pan from heat and allow to cool slightly. Whisk all 6 egg whites very stiffly and fold into yolk mixture. Pour into prepared soufflé dish and bake in hot oven (375° F-400° F or Gas No. 5-6) for 25-30 minutes. Serve immediately.

Suzanne Mahon

ORANGE CARAMEL

*6 large oranges
2 tablespoons cream
2 tablespoons butter
2 tablespoons golden syrup
2 tablespoons brown sugar (optional)
almonds — chopped (optional)*

Slice oranges finely and remove surplus juice. Heat cream, butter, golden syrup and brown sugar together. Add this hot caramel just before serving the fruit. This can also be done with bananas and chopped almonds can also be added.

Helen Leslie

ORANGE FOOL

4 oranges
2 lemons
1 pt cream — whipped
sugar
sponge cakes

FOR GARNISH (OPTIONAL)
almonds — toasted and grated

Grate the rind of 2 oranges and 1 lemon and mix with the juice of the 4 oranges and 2 lemons and the whipped cream. Add sugar to taste. Line a dish with cut up sponge cakes, pour the fool over them and refrigerate for a few hours. Grated toasted almonds can be added to garnish.

Elizabeth Mount Charles

SLIVRE RAISON

Westport House

BANANA PUDDING

> 6 *bananas*
> 1 *oz butter*
> 1 *dessertspoon rum*
> 2 *egg whites — whipped*
> 3 *oz castor sugar*

Slice bananas and put in an oven-dish with the butter. Cook a little until bananas are soft, then add the rum. Add meringue topping made of egg whites whipped with sugar. Put in very slow oven (280° F or Gas No. $\frac{1}{2}$) until meringue is well browned. Serve with cream.

Jennifer Altamont

SPRINGFORT HALL
MALLOW
Co. CORK
S. IRELAND

PEARS IN RED WINE

5-6 ripe eating pears
¼ pt red wine
5 oz lump sugar
rind 1 lemon
small piece cinnamon stick
1 oz browned almonds — shredded
1 teaspoon arrowroot

Put ¼ pt water and the wine in a saucepan and dissolve the sugar while mixing in the flavourings slowly. Bring mixture to the boil and boil for about 1 minute. Peel pears and remove eye from the base but leave on the stalks. Place them with the liquid in a covered pan and poach until tender. Even if the pears are ripe, poach them for at least 20 or 30 minutes to prevent discolouring. Remove pears and strain the syrup which should be reduced to a ½ pt in the cooking. Mix the arrowroot with a little water before adding to the syrup and stir until it boils. Then cook until the liquid is clear (lump sugar gives a crystal-clear liquid). Arrange the pears in a serving dish and spoon over the wine sauce and finish by scattering the browned and shredded almonds on top. Serve with whipped cream on the side.

Hance Cooper

Dunsany Castle, Meath

CHOCOLATE SURPRISE

2 *dozen sponge fingers*
$\frac{1}{2}$ *lb plain chocolate*
4 *eggs*
4 *tablespoons sugar*
4 *tablespoons water*
1 $\frac{1}{2}$ *teaspoons vanilla*

FOR GARNISH
walnuts — chopped

Separate egg yolks from whites and beat lightly. Line a cake-tin (false bottomed) with greaseproof paper coming well over sides of tin. Line bottom and sides with sponge fingers (brown side out). Melt chocolate in double pan, add sugar, water and egg yolks. Cook until smooth, stirring constantly. Cool, add vanilla and fold in beaten egg whites. Pour half the mixture into the tin. Put layer of sponge fingers over the mixture then add remainder of mixture. Cover with greasproof paper. Refrigerate for several hours. Remove from tin and sprinkle with chopped walnuts.

Sheila Dunsany

HUNT BALL CHOCOLATE PUDDING

$\frac{1}{2}$ *lb plain chocolate*
3 eggs
3 tablespoons white sugar
8 trifle sponges

Separate the egg yolks from the whites. Melt chocolate with 3 tablespoons water and cool. Beat sugar and egg yolks in double saucepan, add chocolate and fold in egg whites. Lay sponges in glass dish, cover with the mixture and chill well before serving.

Mother Cusack

HALSEY PUDDING
NELLIE GALLAGHER'S RECIPE

2 eggs
weight of eggs in butter
weight of eggs in flour
weight of one egg in castor sugar
3 tablespoons good strawberry jam
½ teaspoon bicarbonate of soda

SAUCE
2 egg yolks
1 tablespoon castor sugar
1 glass sherry

Beat butter and sugar to a cream. Add eggs one at a time and beat well. Add jam. Lastly add flour and soda. Butter a basin and put mixture in it. Steam for 2 hours. Whip all the sauce ingredients to a froth over hot water until the sauce resembles whipped cream. Serve the pudding with the sauce.

Henry P. McIlhenny

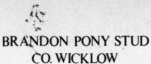

AVOCADO PUDDING

*2 ripe avocados
1 dessertspoon castor sugar
⅓ pt cream — whipped
juice 1 lemon*

Mash avocados with silver fork. Blend well with sugar and lemon juice.
Fold in whipped cream. Chill well for 1 hour.

Deirdre Corbin

FRUIT DUMPLINGS

1 ½ *oz butter*
1 *egg*
pinch salt
6 *oz cottage cheese (home-made if possible)*
½ *lb plain flour*
3 *tablespoons milk*
1 *lb fresh fruit (plums, cherries, apricots or apples)*

Mix well the butter, salt and egg in a basin. Add half the cottage cheese, flour and milk. Make soft (but not sticky) pastry. Roll out lightly to ¼-inch thickness. Cut into 1½-inch squares, put the fruit in the middle, 1 plum or 1 apricot with 4 cherries or 2 pieces of apple. Cover fruit with pastry completely, making sure the fruit is dry before you start to make round dumplings. Dip one by one into boiling salty water and cook for 5–8 minutes. Do not overcook. When ready, lift out one by one, place in a strainer first, then onto a plate, pour hot butter over, sprinkle with castor sugar and garnish with the remaining 3 oz cottage cheese.

Hana Snyder

GLIN CASTLE
CO. LIMERICK
IRELAND.

SUMMER PUDDING
MAI LISTON'S RECIPE

2 *lb loganberries* and/or *raspberries*
6 *slices crustless white bread*
½ *lb sugar*

Wash berries thoroughly and place in saucepan with the sugar — no water. Simmer for 15 minutes. Line a soufflé dish with the bread cut in fingers. When the berries are cold, force them through a sieve and pour the resulting purée over the fingers of bread. Put any remaining bread fingers over the top and press a weighted saucer or plate on the top as a lid. Leave in refrigerator overnight. Serve with whipped cream.

Olda Fitzgerald

TEA ICE CREAM

1 *pt double cream*
$\frac{1}{4}$ *pt very strong cold Indian tea*
4 *oz castor sugar*
4 *egg yolks — well beaten*

Scald cream over low heat. Remove from heat, stir in tea, sugar and beaten egg yolks. Stir all the time and cook over very low heat until the mixture begins to thicken. Sieve and freeze.

Shanes Castle, Antrim

BAKED ALASKA

1 brick best vanilla ice cream
½ lb white grapes
3 egg whites
6 oz castor sugar

Peel the grapes and remove the pips. Spread them on the bottom of a fireproof dish roughly the same size as the ice cream. Beat the egg whites stiffly, adding sugar gradually and beating all the time. Put the dish in a baking tin surrounded by ice cubes. Place the ice cream, which should be as hard as possible, on top of the grapes and cover with the meringue. Bake quickly in a hot oven (450° F or Gas No. 8) for about 3 minutes or until the meringue is golden. Serve at once.

Georgina O'Neill

CHESTNUT PUDDING

1 *medium can sweetened chestnut purée*
4 *tablespoons brandy*
4 *tablespoons sugar*
2 *tablespoons cocoa*
cream for topping

Put chestnut purée, sugar and cocoa in mixer. Add brandy and beat until all are well blended. Put onto dish and shape into a peak. Stiffly whip cream and place on top of peak. Use blunt knife to make cream look like snow drifts.

Donna Maria d'Ardia Caracciolo

CHARLOTTE GRAINNE MAOL

$\frac{1}{2}$ lb sponge finger biscuits
3 egg yolks
$\frac{3}{4}$ oz gelatine
2 oz pineapple — chopped
2 oz cream — whipped
$\frac{1}{2}$ pt milk
$\frac{1}{2}$ glass Irish whiskey
$\frac{1}{2}$ oz cherries
$\frac{1}{2}$ oz angelica

Line the bottom of a charlotte mould with the biscuits trimmed at one end so that they meet in the centre. Line sides of mould with biscuits, tightly packed. Make a custard by bringing the milk to the boil, adding egg yolks and sugar and cooling carefully over low heat. Be sure to whisk all the time. Take off heat and allow to cool. When cool, fill the centre of the mould with the custard and add gelatine dissolved in a little warm water. Add half the whipped cream to the custard just before it sets, with the pineapple flavoured with the whiskey. When set, turn charlotte onto a dish and decorate with the remainder of cream, cherries and angelica.

Nicola O'Reilly

NESTA'S FLAMING PUDDING

1½ lb black grapes
1 pt cream — stiffly whipped
1 sponge flan case
2 glasses brandy
2 tablespoons brown sugar
2 tablespoons chopped almonds

Put flan case on a plate and pour 1 glass brandy over it. Cut the grapes in half, take out the pips and pile the grapes into the flan case, then whip the cream very stiff and cover the complete flan as if you were icing a cake. Put in refrigerator to chill. Lightly toast the chopped almonds and when they have cooled mix them with the brown sugar. Just before serving the flan, sprinkle with the nuts and sugar. Heat the remaining glass of brandy until it flares and pour it over the lot. Try to get it to the table while still flaming. (The cheaper the brandy, the better it burns.)

WHISKEY PARFAIT

4 eggs
3 oz castor sugar
2 tablespoons Irish whiskey
2 oz flaked toasted almonds
¼ pt double cream — whipped
1 oz mixed peel

Put egg yolks and sugar into large bowl, beat well with a wooden spoon until light and creamy. Stir in whiskey and almonds. Fold cream and stiffly beaten egg whites into whiskey mixture. Blend gently but thoroughly. Rinse 2-pt mould or ring mould with cold water. Sprinkle mould with mixed peel and pour in mixture. Chill well. Turn out by dipping the mould in boiling water for a second.

[signature]

IRISH COFFEE JELLY

$\frac{3}{4}$ *pt very strong coffee*
2 *level tablespoons castor sugar*
$\frac{1}{2}$ *oz powdered gelatine*
$\frac{1}{4}$ *pt Irish whiskey*
$\frac{1}{2}$ *pt double cream*

Put the coffee into a pan with the sugar and gelatine and heat almost, but not quite, to boiling, stirring all the time until sugar and gelatine are dissolved. Take the pan off the stove, stir in the whiskey, then share the coffee between 4 $\frac{1}{2}$ - pt glasses and put into the refrigerator to set. Before serving, top with cream.

Pamela Gormanston

SNAFFLES,
47, LOWER LEESON STREET,
DUBLIN 2.
DUBLIN 60790

MUSHROOM FRITTERS WITH TARTARE SAUCE

25 mushrooms
deep fat for frying
½ pt tartare sauce (see page 193)
frying batter (see PANCAKE BATTER RECIPE *page 212)*

Wipe mushrooms and slice off end of stalk leaving the neck intact. Dip in frying batter. Plunge into hot fat (390° F) until crisp. Drain well and serve with tartare sauce.

CHEESE BALLS

6 egg whites
10 oz gruyère cheese — freshly grated
fine breadcrumbs
deep fat for frying
3 oz parmesan cheese — finely grated

Cheese balls must be made at the last moment and should be served immediately.

Beat egg whites very stiffly. Fold in grated gruyère cheese. Make small balls of the mixture. Roll in fine breadcrumbs and plunge into hot fat (400° F) until golden brown. Drain on paper and serve immediately. Sprinkle the grated parmesan cheese on top.

COLD CHEESE SAVOURY

½ pt cream
2 eggs
3 oz cheese — grated
cayenne pepper to taste
salt to taste

Whip cream and eggs with a little cayenne pepper and salt. Add grated cheese. Put the mixture in a greased fireproof dish. Put dish in deep baking tin containing a little cold water. Bake in moderate oven (about 350° F or Gas No. 4) for about 15 minutes or until set. Put in refrigerator to cool.

Bunny McCalmont

CHEESE RAMEKIN

4 oz breadcrumbs
½ pt milk
1 teaspoon French mustard
2 eggs
2 oz cheese — grated
salt and pepper

Boil milk and soak breadcrumbs in the hot milk for a few minutes. Add mustard, grated cheese, seasoning and 2 egg yolks. Mix well. Whip egg whites stiffly and add to soft mixture. Put into ramekins and bake for ½ hour at 400° F or Gas No. 6.

Jessica Rathdonnell

TOASTED CHEESE EMLAGHMORE

1 *lb cheddar cheese — grated*
8 *slices brown toast*
½ *pt brown ale*
1 *glass brandy*
½ *teaspoon ginger*
½ *teaspoon mace*
1 *dessertspoon demerara sugar*

Melt grated cheese in oven in serving dish. Meanwhile heat brown ale and brandy with ginger and mace. Dip pieces of toast in this mixture, cover with sugar and ladle on melted cheese. The mulled ale can be drunk afterwards.

OYSTERS WITH FENNEL

24 *unopened oysters*
$\frac{1}{4}$ *lb butter*
10 *fennel leaves — finely chopped*
8 *wedges lemon*

Scrub and wash the oysters. Roast them in very hot oven (450° F or Gas No. 8) for about 10 minutes just until the shells open. Melt the butter and sprinkle oysters with fennel. Serve in the shell, with the hot melted butter and wedges of lemon.

BACON CRISPS
MAY A. CARROLL'S RECIPE

$\frac{1}{2}$ *lb very thin streaky bacon rashers*
2 eggs — beaten
soft white breadcrumbs
deep fat for frying

Dip rashers in egg and then breadcrumbs. Fry in deep fat until crisp.

Padraic Colpoer Trench

SALMON LIVERS ON TOAST

4 salmon livers
salt
black peppercorns — freshly ground
4 slices hot brown toast
1 oz butter

Fry the salmon livers very gently in butter for about 2 minutes each side, until cooked but still pink inside. Serve on slices of toast and pour excess butter over the top.

VINAIGRETTE DRESSING

4 tablespoons good olive oil
1 tablespoon wine vinegar
½ teaspoon salt
black peppercorns — freshly ground

Place vinegar, salt and pepper in salad bowl. Mix well to dissolve salt. Add olive oil, mixing well.

FRENCH DRESSING WITH CREAM

½ teaspoon salt
black peppercorns — freshly ground
4 tablespoons double cream
1 dessertspoon white wine vinegar

Place vinegar, salt and pepper in a bowl. Mix well to dissolve salt. Add cream gradually, until mixed well.

VINAIGRETTE DRESSING FOR MEAT

Basic vinaigrette dressing recipe, as above, plus:
1 tablespoon capers
1 tablespoon parsley — finely chopped
2 spring onions — finely chopped

Mix all ingredients well. This is excellent with lambs' tongues and cold boiled beef.

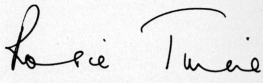

AIOLI SAUCE

4 cloves garlic
2 egg yolks
salt and black pepper
½ pt good olive oil
2 teaspoons lemon juice

Pound the garlic in a mortar with salt and pepper to an oily consistency. Mix the egg yolks in well and start adding the oil very slowly with a wooden spoon, as if making mayonnaise beating constantly. Add a little lemon juice from time to time. If the sauce starts to curdle, add a few drops of lukewarm water to it and whisk vigorously. It is excellent served with raw or cooked vegetables or fish.

SNAFFLES,
47, LOWER LEESON STREET,
DUBLIN 2.
DUBLIN 60790

TARTARE SAUCE

$\frac{1}{2}$ *pt mayonnaise*
2 tablespoons capers
2 gherkins
1 tablespoon parsley — finely chopped
2 spring onions
dash of fresh lemon juice — optional
salt and pepper

Chop capers, gherkins, parsley and spring onions very finely. Mix well with mayonnaise. Season well and add dash of lemon juice if liked.

TARRAGON SAUCE

$\frac{1}{2}$ pt dry white wine
3 sprigs tarragon
2 oz butter
1 tablespoon flour
$\frac{1}{4}$ pt good chicken stock
salt and pepper

Reduce the wine by half by boiling. Add leaves of 2 of the sprigs of tarragon and let stand over low heat until odour of tarragon is quite strong. Chop the leaves of the remaining tarragon sprig. Make a roux with the butter and flour, add stock, salt and pepper and stir well. When smooth, add wine and tarragon mixture and cool very gently without letting it thicken. Before serving, strain sauce and add chopped tarragon leaves. A delicious sauce over poached chicken, fish or eggs.

SNAFFLES,
47, LOWER LEESON STREET,
DUBLIN 2.
DUBLIN 60790

QUICK HOLLANDAISE SAUCE

1 lb butter
6 egg yolks
dash of lemon juice
pepper to taste

Melt the butter. Put egg yolks in liquidiser and slowly pour on very hot butter while blending at highest speed. Add lemon juice and pepper. Check seasoning. (If Irish butter is used, salt will not be necessary.) Keep warm by storing in a thermos flask for a few hours. Very good for fish, especially salmon.

Carton House, Kildare

SHRIMP SAUCE

2 oz butter
1 tablespoon flour
¼ pt stock
¼ pt white wine
about 10 green grapes — skinned and chopped
1 small tin shrimps
salt and pepper
fennel — chopped (optional)

Melt butter and stir in flour, add stock (the liquid from the shrimps will do) and white wine, and stir until the sauce begins to thicken. Add the shrimps and the chopped grapes. Season, stir and serve. A little chopped fennel can be added, if liked. Serve with any fish dish.

NORMANDY SAUCE

1½ oz butter
2 oz flour
½ pt fish stock
½ pt double cream
2 egg yolks
1-2 tablespoons lemon juice
salt and pepper

Make a roux with butter and flour, cook for a few minutes and stir in fish stock. Blend the cream with the egg yolks. When the roux starts to thicken, remove from heat. Season with salt and pepper. Add the cream and egg mixture and stir until well mixed. Add lemon juice according to taste and check seasoning. Keep warm over hot water without further cooking. This is an excellent sauce for fish or chicken dishes.

TOMATO SAUCE
NELLIE GALLAGHER'S RECIPE

2 oz butter
1 onion — chopped
1 bay leaf
$\frac{1}{3}$ pt sour cream
2 tablespoons celery — chopped
2 tablespoons vinegar
sprig thyme
3 tomatoes — fresh or canned
3 tablespoons tomato paste
2 tablespoons carrot — chopped
salt and pepper

Cook onion with tomatoes and celery for 15 minutes. Add other ingredients except sour cream and cook for 20 minutes. Put through a fine sieve or blender. Replace in saucepan and bring to boil. Add sour cream.

SOUR CREAM SAUCE

1 onion — finely chopped
2 cloves garlic — finely chopped
4 oz butter
1 oz flour
2 teaspoons horseradish
1 glass white wine
$\frac{3}{4}$ pt sour cream
salt and pepper

Lightly fry onion and garlic in the butter until they begin to soften. Shake in flour and stir until the flour has absorbed the butter, pour in the wine and stir until smooth; a little more wine or some water can be added if it seems too thick. Lower heat and stir in horseradish and sour cream. Season. Cook for about 5 minutes over low heat and serve hot with roast beef.

GAME GRAVY

1 *carcase of large game bird*
   or 2 *carcases of small game birds*
1 *oz butter*
1 *onion — chopped*
1 *glass sherry*
2 *pt good chicken stock*
sprig thyme
sprig marjoram
2 *dessertspoons parsley — chopped*
1 *bay leaf*
salt and pepper

Pound carcases and sauté gently in butter with onion and herbs. Add seasoning. Add stock and simmer for 1 hour until stock is reduced by half. Strain, remove fat and add sherry.

VENISON SAUCE

6 shallots — finely chopped
6 onions — finely chopped
2 carrots — finely chopped
$\frac{1}{2}$ pt wine vinegar
2 sprigs parsley — chopped
1 small bay leaf
2 teaspoons salt
pinch cayenne pepper
2 oz butter
3 oz flour
$\frac{1}{2}$ pt marinade (from the venison)
1 teaspoon sugar
2 dessertspoons Chartreuse liqueur

Simmer shallots, onions and carrots with the vinegar, parsley, bay leaf, salt and cayenne pepper over gentle heat for 1 hour. Brown butter and blend in flour. Stir in about $\frac{1}{2}$ pt marinade in which the venison has been marinating. Purée the vegetables, mix with the sugar and add to the marinade mixture. Simmer for $\frac{1}{2}$ hour. 10 minutes before serving add the Chartreuse. Strain sauce into a sauce bowl.

COLONEL HAWKER'S SAUCE

2 glasses port
1 tablespoon bottled barbecue sauce
1 tablespoon mushroom ketchup
1 tablespoon lemon juice
1 oz butter
¾ oz flour
small pinch cayenne pepper
pinch mace
2 cloves
½ pt strong consommé or *game stock*
1 shallot

Stew shallot, cayenne pepper, mace, cloves and stock for 20 minutes. Add port and bring to the boil. In another saucepan make a roux with the butter and flour and add the stock sauce, barbecue sauce, mushroom ketchup and lemon juice. Cook slowly, stirring all the time, until the consistency of thin cream. Serve with wildfowl.

Betty Caroline Laidlaw

HORSERADISH SAUCE

4 *teaspoons Dijon mustard*
4 *teaspoons white wine vinegar*
2 *tablespoons fresh horseradish — grated*
1 *tablespoon castor sugar*
pinch salt
6 *tablespoons double cream*
2 *oz soft breadcrumbs*

Mix the mustard and vinegar in a bowl. When well mixed add the remaining ingredients and mix well. Very good with hare, rabbit and pork.

PIQUANTE SAUCE

1 *shallot — finely chopped*
4 *tablespoons red wine vinegar*
1 *sugar lump*
1 $\frac{1}{2}$ *oz butter*
1 *oz flour*
$\frac{1}{2}$ *pt stock*
2 *tablespoons pickles — chopped*
salt and pepper

Put shallot in a saucepan with vinegar and sugar. Heat until vinegar is reduced by half. Heat butter in another saucepan until it turns brown. Add the flour and stir until brown. Stir in stock, and when it begins to thicken season with salt and pepper. Add the vinegar mixture and stir until it reaches the desired thickness. It should not be too thick. Strain before serving and add the pickles. May be served with tongue, pigs' feet or snipe.

CUMBERLAND SAUCE

1 ½ pt jar good redcurrant jelly
1 orange — juice and grated rind
1 lemon — grated rind
1 dessertspoon worcester sauce
1 dessertspoon good chutney sauce
pepper to taste
1 glass port

Put all ingredients in saucepan and heat slowly until at boiling point. Simmer gently for 10 minutes. Strain and cool. Store in airtight jar in cool place. Very good with ham and tongue.

QUICK COLD MUSTARD SAUCE

$\frac{1}{2}$ *pt sour cream*
2 tablespoons Dijon mustard

Stir mustard into sour cream and serve. Goes well with tongue, pigs' feet etc.

HOT MUSTARD SAUCE

1 *egg yolk*
1 *teaspoon vinegar*
2 *teaspoons French mustard*
3 *oz soft butter*
pinch cayenne pepper
salt to taste

Add the mustard to the egg yolk and beat lightly with the vinegar in the top of a small double boiler over simmering water. The sauce must *never* boil. When it begins to thicken add the butter bit by bit, beating all the time. If the sauce should separate, remove from the heat and beat in vigorously a tablespoon of iced water. When the sauce is blended, remove from the heat and season with salt and cayenne pepper. Pour over tongue, cold meat or pigs' feet.

Bishop's Court, Kildare

SNAFFLES,
47, LOWER LEESON STREET,
DUBLIN 2.
DUBLIN 60790

BRANDY SAUCE

1 ½ *pt good chicken* or *veal stock*
1 *carrot — coarsely chopped*
2 *medium onions — coarsely chopped*
1 *clove garlic — crushed*
1 *stick celery — chopped*
3 *oz butter*
2 *oz flour*
¼ *pt dry vermouth*
1 *glass brandy*
sprig parsley
sprig thyme
2 *tablespoons cream*
salt and pepper to taste

Sweat onions, garlic, carrot and celery in butter. Stir in flour and cook until golden brown. Add stock, blending well. Add salt, pepper, parsley, thyme and vermouth and simmer very gently until sauce has reduced by a quarter. Add brandy and cook for a further 10 minutes. Strain and stir in cream. Check seasoning. This sauce should be served with pigeon or game dishes. It is particularly good with chicken breasts in puff pastry.

MARMALADE SAUCE

2 oz butter
1 oz flour
juice 1 orange
1 teaspoon orange peel — grated
3 tablespoons marmalade
1 glass sweet vermouth or *sherry*
a few sultanas

Melt butter in pan and stir in flour, then stir in orange juice and marmalade. Add orange peel, sultanas and vermouth. Stir until the sauce begins to thicken. Serve hot over ice cream. This sauce is also very good with duck if you use the grated rind of 2 oranges and less marmalade.

OYSTER STUFFING
MAY A. CARROLL'S RECIPE

8 oz breadcrumbs
12 fresh oysters
1 egg
4 oz butter
1 red or green pepper — very finely chopped
juice ½ lemon
rind 1 lemon — finely grated
1 teaspoon onion — chopped
1 teaspoon parsley — chopped
good chicken stock to bind
salt and pepper to taste

Combine all ingredients, adding stock to make the right consistency. This stuffing is suitable for fowl or fish.

PANCAKES

3 oz butter
4 oz plain flour — sifted
$\frac{1}{2}$ pt milk
2 eggs
1 teaspoon salt or sugar

Put flour in a bowl. Add milk gradually, stirring constantly with wooden spoon so that the batter will be thin without lumps. Break eggs into batter and beat until well blended. Add salt or sugar. Melt butter and add to batter. Let the batter rest in refrigerator for 2 hours at least before using. (Makes about 10 pancakes).

POTATO CAKES

$\frac{1}{2}$ *lb cold potatoes — mashed*
1 *oz margarine*
3 *oz flour*
1 *teaspoon salt*

Melt margarine and mix mashed potatoes. Add salt and work the flour in. Roll out paste into thin sheet. Cut out desired shapes. Put on hot griddle for about 3 minutes each side. Serve hot with butter.

Mountbatten of Burma

MY GRANDMOTHER'S SCONES

8 oz self-raising flour
or plain flour
2 heaped teaspoons baking powder
¼ teaspoon salt
1 teaspoon sugar (optional)
1 egg
½ pt milk

Thoroughly grease 12 bun tins. Sift flour, baking powder, salt, and sugar (if desired) into basin. Beat egg and milk together and pour into flour. Mix very thoroughly. The mixture should be very creamy and not at all dry. Drop small spoonfuls into greased tins and bake in a very hot oven (450°-500° F or Gas No. 8-9) for 10-15 minutes until well risen and brown. Very quick and easy to make as these scones involve no rolling or cutting.

Suzanne Mahon

GINGERBREAD
MAY A. CARROLL'S RECIPE

1 lb flour
$\frac{1}{2}$ lb butter
1 dessertspoon allspice
1 dessertspoon ground ginger
2 teaspoons bicarbonate of soda
$\frac{1}{2}$ lb mixed nuts
1 egg — beaten
$\frac{1}{2}$ lb black treacle
$\frac{1}{2}$ lb brown sugar

Dissolve butter, treacle, sugar and add other ingredients, leaving the nuts and egg until last. The soda should be well blended with the flour. Bake in flat greased tin in the oven (225-250° F, Gas No. $\frac{1}{2}$-1) until firm to touch (about 1 hour).

FOOLPROOF MERINGUES FOR SHAPES

4 egg whites
½ lb castor sugar
pinch salt

Beat egg whites lightly and put with sugar, salt and 2 tablespoons boiling water into top of double boiler (or basin in hot water). Bring nearly to boil, but never to boiling point. Beat mixture while it is heating. When meringue is firm and holds its shape, remove from heat and whisk a minute or two more. Have ready oiled greaseproof paper and place shapes, as desired, on it. Bake at 250° F or Gas No. ¼ until firm (time for cooking will depend on size of shapes).

PORTER CAKE

1 lb plain flour
¾ lb butter
¾ lb soft brown sugar
1 bottle stout
1 teaspoon bicarbonate of soda
rind 1 lemon
3 eggs — well beaten
1 ½ lb mixed fruit
¼ lb mixed peel
1 teaspoon mixed spice
1 teaspoon cinnamon
a little nutmeg

Sift flour, rub butter into flour until it resembles fine breadcrumbs. Add all the dry ingredients, except bicarbonate of soda. Warm the stout, add bicarbonate of soda and then pour on beaten eggs, mixing well. Add to the flour mixture slowly, and beat for 15 minutes. Bake in a very moderate oven (325° F or Gas No. 3) for 3 hours. The cake should not be cut for 1 week.

GUINNESS CAKE

$\frac{1}{2}$ lb butter
$\frac{1}{2}$ lb soft brown sugar
4 eggs
10 oz plain flour
$\frac{1}{2}$ lb seedless raisins
$\frac{1}{2}$ lb sultanas
2 level teaspoons mixed spice
4 oz mixed peel
4 oz walnuts — chopped
4 oz cherries — chopped
1 pt Guinness

Cream the butter and sugar together until light and creamy. Gradually beat in the eggs. Fold in the flour and mixed spice. Add the raisins, sultanas, mixed peel, cherries and walnuts. Mix well together. Stir 4 tablespoons of Guinness into the mixture and mix well. Turn into a prepared 7-inch round cake tin and bake in a very moderate oven (325° F or Gas No. 3) for 1 hour. Then reduce heat to a cool oven 300° F or Gas No. 2) and cook for another 1$\frac{1}{2}$ hours. Allow to cool. Remove from tin. Prick the base of the cake with a skewer, and spoon over the remainder of the Guinness. Keep the cake 1 week. If you like, before eating spoon over 8 tablespoons of Guinness again into the base of the cake.

Miranda Iveagh

INDEX